"And now here is my secret,
a very simple secret;
it is only with the heart that one can see properly;
what is essential is invisible to the eye"

Antoine de Saint-Exupery, 1900 - 1944
French novelist and aviator

Lucky Duck Statement

The Heart Masters books were sent to us from Australia. We not only liked the content but the Vision Statement. These books seemed to promote emotional intelligence in a style very similar to Lucky Ducks approach. Apart from minor changes to particular Australian references, these books follow the original format.

ISBN: 1 904 315 02 X

Published by Lucky Duck Publishing Ltd.
3 Thorndale Mews, Clifton, Bristol BS8 2HX, UK

www.luckyduck.co.uk

Commissioning Editor: George Robinson

Printed in the UK by The Book Factory, Mildmay Avenue, London N1 4RS, UK

First published by:
Dandenong, Victoria, Australia

Lay out: Patricia Headford

Illustrations: Patricia Headford, Gary Shaw, Lianne Gough

Inyahead Vision Statement

We aim to provide educationally based programs and training that promote well-being and resilience, and are characterised by creativity, excitement, integrity, fun and collaborative relationships

Underlying Principles

The following principles guide and inform all of our work:

➤   A shared vision and commitment to people

➤   A sensitivity to the stages of development in people's lives

➤   A commitment to supportive relationships

Beliefs

School is a community.

People seek meaning in what they do.

Everyone is a leader.

Trust is essential for building confidence.

Learning should be fun.

A culture of belonging is essential.

Opportunities for meaningful contribution and participation build resilience.

Optimistic thinking is a skill not an inheritance.

A diversity of coping strategies is desirable.

Recognition builds meaning.

Contents

Classroom Sessions

Evaluation Tools

Awards Ideas & Puzzles

Personal Best Programme

Introduction and Rationale

Emotional intelligence is the ability to understand and manage your own emotions and those of others. It involves being aware of what you are feeling and having some capacity to regulate how you respond to those feelings. It also encompasses being able to empathise with other people and relate to them sensitively and appropriately. Emotional intelligence is a critical factor in determining the quality of your personal life, career and educational success.

Emotional intelligence makes a major contribution to the development of resilience - the happy knack of being able to bunji jump through the pitfalls of life. A sense of belonging in the family, with peers and at school is more easily achieved if self-awareness and self-belief are nurtured together with learning how to tune into the feelings of others and to relate positively in social situations.

The skills of emotional intelligence and resilience can be taught and developed in young people. Not only do they provide a powerful way of protecting young people from harm, they also promote the skills that lead to success in social and organisational settings.

This package contains 20 weekly sessions for the middle to senior years of primary school. Each session is designed in such a way as to introduce a critical skill and to provide some knowledge and awareness about those skills. Attached to each session is a "habit builder". While knowledge and awareness can lead to attitude change, the development of habits is a more powerful way of creating enduring behavioural change. Where possible it is desirable to make each session become a weekly theme.

Essentially the package is designed to develop the key aspects of emotional intelligence and resilience which include:

1. The ability to read and take into consideration the feelings of others

2. An awareness of our own feelings

3. The ability to regulate or calm our feelings

4. Proficiency in a range of social competencies

5. The skills and opportunities that enhance a sense of belonging.

How to Use this Book

This programme is based on research with Australian students and the factors that assist with their development of resilience and emotional intelligence. It has been trialled in Australian schools.

The programme is divided into 20 sessions. While each session is designed to last for one hour with a core activity, discussion questions, a worksheet and a habit builder, the length of lessons will depend on the approach of teachers and the response of students. Some teachers will spend longer periods of time developing activities, understanding and skills. Some may even wish to add supplementary activities and to expand on sessions they consider important. Other teachers may prefer to develop their own programmes and only use some sessions, and others again may only wish to use specific sessions for a specific purpose or in response to a specific incident.

The core activity is at the beginning of each session. It attempts to provide an experience for students that they may use for reflection on when completing the discussion questions and the worksheets.

The habit builder activity is an activity students do away from the classroom. It may be reflective or it may be experiential. It is intended to encourage students to apply the classroom programme beyond the specific session.

In addition, a variety of warm up activities are provided on pages 10-13. These activities may be either useful to focus attention, build trust, have fun, help all students to become involved or simply to help energise everyone.

ACKNOWLEDGEMENTS

Original Front Cover Design: Yabby Graphics
Layout: Patricia Headford
Illustrations: Gary Shaw, Lianne Gough and Patricia Headford

Thank you to the following schools for contributing to the development of this resource

Wesley Preparatory School
Howard Springs Primary School
Park Hill Primary School
Queenscliff Primary School

Wonderful Warm Ups

Wonderful Warm Ups

The 'Wonderful Warm Up' activities can be used for a variety of reasons. They may be used as an experiential way of developing an understanding, to energise, to encourage everybody to join in, because they are relevant to a lesson for some reason, or simply for a bit of fun. They can also be adjusted according to the age and needs of the group.

Active Games

Group Juggling

Ask students to break into three groups (of at least six students). Give a ball to each group. Instruct each group that they must keep the ball constantly moving. They must also stop the ball from touching the floor. The team that can do this the longest is the victor.

To add interest or another level of difficulty, especially with larger groups, extra balls could be added so that a group has two or three balls circulating at the one time.

Another variation is for the student with the ball to throw it into the air and call a student's name. That student runs into the middle of the circle and catches the ball then repeats the process.

Common Chaos

Ask for a volunteer. Everybody else sits in a circle on a seat. The volunteer thinks of a common characteristic and calls it out. All those students to whom it applies jump up out of their seat and run to another seat on the other side of the circle. The initial volunteer also runs to a seat. The last person standing goes into the middle and calls out another characteristic.

Some examples are:

➢ Everybody who likes ice cream.

➢ All of the boys or girls.

➢ Everybody who plays sport.

➢ Everybody who is smiling.

➢ Everybody who had toast for breakfast.

Wonderful Warm Ups...cont

Playful Games

No Laughing Please

Everybody sits in a circle apart from one volunteer. The volunteer looks around the circle and chooses a likely target. The volunteer then tries to make the target laugh. The volunteer can do most things besides really gross things such as swearing, touching or taking off clothes. Pull faces, make jokes, do somersaults, look up noses, blow kisses, say I love you..... anything! The target must look straight into the volunteer's eyes while trying not to laugh.

I Don't Believe It!

Get students to make up one, two or three true things about themselves and one fib. They should try to make the fib sound believable. The rest of the class can ask questions, and the 'fibber' can either answer them honestly or dishonestly. The rest of the class, or a panel, has to guess the fib.

A variation on this activity, is to get students to answer 5 or more questions about themselves. Favourite food, sport, subject, colour etc. Then put all of the answers into a box. Pull one set of answers out at a time and the rest of the class tries to guess who it is.

Slave Auction

In pairs or groups get students to make up an advertisement to sell one of the group members naming all of their positive attributes and why they would be a good buy. Give examples like 'Nike's - Just Do It' and Toyota's - 'Oh what a feeling!'

It Drives Me Nuts

Each student takes turns in standing up and telling everybody what drives them nuts.

After each statement, everybody has a group scream in empathy.

Wonderful Warm Ups...cont

Playful Games

Perfect Parents

Make an advertisement for the perfect parents. Present it to the class.

There's a Time and a Place

Ask for three volunteers. Give each one an inappropriate implement to perform a task. For example, give one student a spade, another a saw and another a fork. Then give each of them an apple and ask them to cut it into four equal pieces.

Who Got It?

Put a bell or a chime in the centre of the circle. All students cover their eyes. Touch a student on the shoulder and they creep into the middle of the room and pick up the bell as quietly as possible. They place the bell behind their back. The teacher nominates a student to guess who took the bell.

THE HEART MASTERS 14

Classroom Sessions

Bunji jumping through life

Purpose

To help students understand the concept of resilience.

Preparation

1.   Locate materials to make a resilience bracelet for each student: an assortment of coloured balls of cotton or wool (at least five) that should be cut into lengths.

2.   Develop a method for twisting or plaiting 5 strands into a cord and tying or looping them to make a bracelet.

     Suggestion: *This may be done by twisting 5 strands until they form a tightly bound cord. Double the cord over half way down and thread it back through the loop. The bracelet can then be tightened around your wrist.*

3.   Photocopy 'Five Skills of Resilience' hand out, 'The Resilience Bracelet' worksheet, 'Bunji' worksheet and the 'Resilience Building' habit builder.

Core Activity

Resilience Bracelet

1. Ask each student to choose five strands of cotton or wool.

2. Instruct all students how to make a bracelet.

3. Explain this is a special bracelet that they should keep for at least the length of this programme. It is to remind them of the special things they are about to learn.

4. Alternatively, the strands of wool can be made into a book mark or an embroidery.

5. Introduce the concept of resilience - resilience is the happy knack of being able to bunji jump through the pitfalls of life.

6. Ask who knows what bunji jumping is?

7. Get students to describe it.

8. Ask students to think about how bunji jumping is like life. e.g. When tough things happen we need to have the skills to bounce back.

9. Make a list of the skills that help people 'bounce back'.

10. Read a fairy tale such as Cinderella or Oliver Twist to illustrate how we need to bounce back or tell a story from your own life.

11. Introduce 5 Skills of Resilience (see page 20 for explanations):
    - ➤ Planning
    - ➤ Energy
    - ➤ Calming
    - ➤ Courage
    - ➤ Caring

12. Explain how we need to practise these skills every day of our lives. They are skills that we learn. The 'Resilience Bracelet' will remind us that we need to practise.

13. Complete the 'Resilience Bracelet' worksheet.

14. Ask students to share with the class the people they know who represent each skill. Ask them to explain why they think these people have this skill.

15. Design a mix of ingredients for a Resilience Remedy. This could include things to make you feel good, friends and people you can rely on, food you like or anything else.

16. Distribute 'The Resilience Building' habit builder and complete with students. (This habit builder works best when students are followed up consistently on a one to one basis.)

Discussion questions

What weakens the power of the bracelet - tiredness, lack of concentration, worrying, loneliness, sadness, fear and confusion?

What might you need for a Resilience Bracelet Repair Kit - the five main threads plus one mystery golden thread?

What power could be in this golden thread?

Who could be specialist bracelet repairers to consult when you are worn out or really cut up - mum/ dad. grandma/pa, aunty/uncle, friend, parents of a friend?

What else can the bracelet do - catch a passing cloud, time travel back and forward, support someone else who needs help until their rope is repaired?

<❖>

The Secret Wisdom
of
The Resilience Bracelet

Planning: doing important things first, developing self control, thinking ahead.

Energy:

developing the habit of doing your best, of persistence, and of overcoming difficulty.

Calming: developing the habit of thinking about your own behaviour and the behaviour of others, and of being able to control your feelings.

Courage: developing the habit of overcoming fear and of behaving fairly and thoughtfully.

Caring: developing habits of personal hygiene, being your own best friend, speaking up for yourself, and thinking about the feelings of other people.

The Resilience Bracelet

1. Trace your hand.

2. On each finger write a skill of resilience.

3. Think of five people you know who have one of the skills of resilience.

4. Write their names beside your hand and draw arrows from each finger to the person with that skill.

What a beautiful hand you have.

Unjumble the thought from Bunji.

Uyo ttemar

BUNJI

Bunji is good at bouncing back up after being down.

Bunji is our jumper!

What do you think Bunji looks like?

Do a drawing of Bunji.

Resilience Building

A resilience skill I want to improve is:

....
....
....

I will start improving my resilience skill by

....
....
....

My diary of the things I do to practise this skill

....
....
....
....
....
....
....

Signed   Signed

....
Student   Teacher

Session TWO

THE GAME SEARCH

Purpose

This session helps students to become more inclusive. This session helps students to clarify acceptable and unacceptable behaviour.

Preparation

➢ Strong piece of rope for game of 'Test of Strength'.

➢ Photocopy 'Being Friendly & Being Mean' worksheet.

➢ Poster paper.

➢ Large paper for posters.

Core Activities

1. **Play the 'Common Chaos' game**

    ➢ Ask for a volunteer. Everybody else sits in a circle on a chair with the volunteer in the centre of the circle.

    ➢ The volunteer thinks of a common characteristic and calls it out.

    ➢ All those students to whom it applies jump up out of their seat and move to another seat on the other side of the circle. The initial volunteer also runs to a seat. Players cannot move to a seat next to them.

    ➢ The person who misses out on a seat stands in the middle and calls out another characteristic, and the game goes on.

    Some examples are:
    a. Everybody who likes ice cream.
    b. All of the boys or girls.
    c. Everybody who plays sport.
    d. Everybody who is smiling.

2. **Play the 'Test of Strength' game.**

    (Use a thick rope that cannot break the skin. Ensure students do not loop the rope around their hands or torso.)

    ➢ Appoint two leaders.

    ➢ Explain you are going to have a test of strength.

    ➢ Ask the leaders to choose four other players each.

    ➢ Place a marker on the floor in a cleared space. Lay the rope over it with equal lengths on either side of the marker.

    ➢ Instruct each team to pick the rope up and hold it tightly.

    ➢ Explain that once the instruction has been given to begin, the point of the game is to tug on the rope until you pull the other team over the line.

    ➢ When one game is finished, choose another two leaders who must choose from the remaining students. Repeat the process until everyone has had a turn.

3. Form students into groups.

4. Distribute 'Being Friendly and Being Mean' worksheet.

5. Make posters of friendly and unfriendly behaviour and pin them up on the wall.

6. Inform students about the 'Games Hunt'.

7. Use the 'Games Search' to choose games for the Party Club celebration (session 9).

Discussion questions

How did students in the first team of 'Test of Strength' feel when they were chosen to participate?

What did students who were not chosen in the first team think to themselves?

Did their thoughts affect their feelings?

Are games more fun when everybody joins in (inclusive games) or when only a few are chosen (exclusive games)?

Is it always possible to be inclusive?

———————————— ◄◆► ————————————

THE GAME SEARCH

Have a games hunt.

Search the school, your homes and your minds for all the games you can find.

Make a class collection.

Explain how to play the games so everybody understands.

Make a list of the games that everybody can play.

Choose a game for each day of the week.

For one week, at a set time each day, the class plays the 'friendly' game.

Being Friendly & Being Mean

Make up poster pictures of **FRIENDLY** behaviour, and **MEAN** behaviour.

Which behaviour do you prefer?

Is your behaviour mostly 'friendly' or mostly 'mean'?

Name calling	/	compliments
Mean comments	/	Nice comments
Hitting	/	Hugging
Ignoring	/	Saying 'Hello'
Hiding	/	Inviting to play

Discover the thought from Bunji by solving the riddle.

To locate something you were looking for   _ I _ _

                                                                                    YOUR

It beats inside your chest   _ E _ _ _

MAGIC & MONSTERS

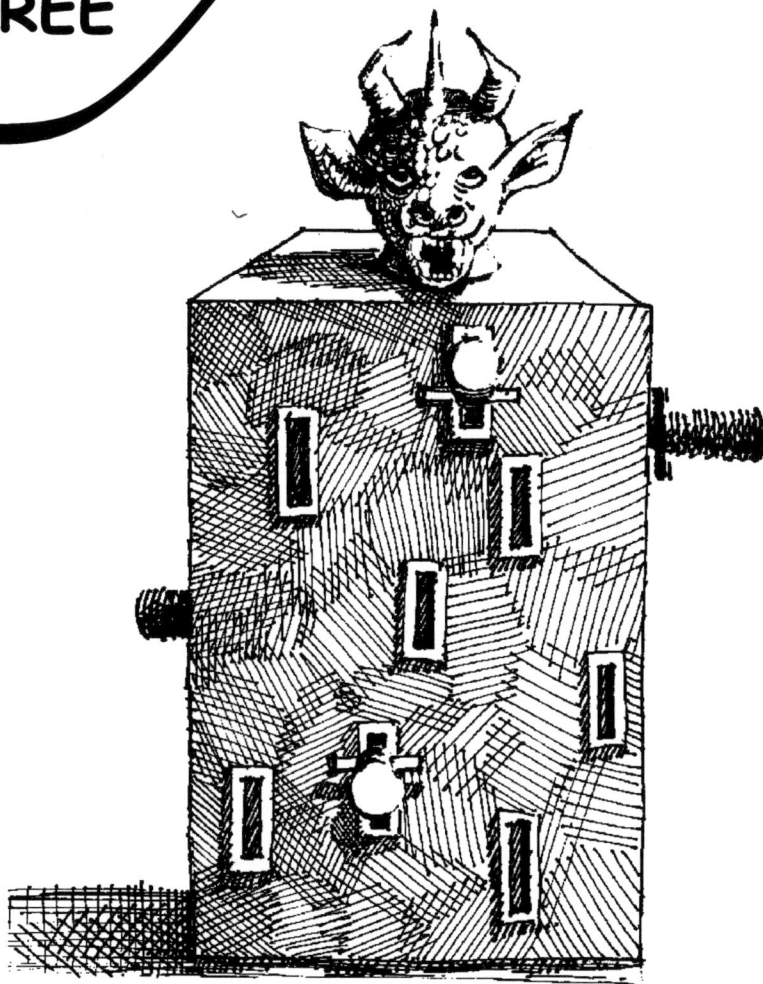

Teachers Notes...........

Purpose

This session helps students to develop team work.

Preparation

1. Find a prop to act as a magic wand and a magic lantern.

2. Collect large sheets of cardboard for groups of 5-7.

3. Photocopy the Pleasant Events handout & 'Let's Do it' worksheet.

Core Activity

1. **Play the 'Magic Wand' game**

    ➤ Mark out a confined space.

    ➤ Choose a volunteer. Give them a soft magic wand and place a magic lantern in a box or in some other defined space.

    ➤ The rest of the students are wizards. Their aim is to get the magic lantern, while the magician must try to protect the lantern. When a wizard is touched with the magic wand they must freeze. The point of the game is for the magician to freeze everybody, and for the wizards to get the magic lantern.

2. **Play the 'Monster' game**

    ➤ Take students into the school grounds or clear a space in the class room.

    ➤ Ask students to form into groups of 5-7, and give each group a piece of cardboard.

    ➤ Identify a point where students must reach to win the game. It could be a tree if outside or some other marker.

    ➤ Ask for a volunteer to be the 'monster' who calls out 'I'm hungry'.

    ➤ The aim of the game is to reach the marker without being eaten by the monster. Without touching anyone, the monster stalks the players and calls out 'I'm hungry!'. On hearing this, the players must immediately drop the cardboard and all stand on it. If a team is last to stand on the cardboard twice in a row, they are out. If anyone falls off, they are exposed and eaten by the monster. Each time the monster calls out, 'I'm hungry', and a team stands on its cardboard, they must halve the size of the cardboard before proceeding. The successful team is the one that reaches the marker first.

3. Return to the classroom. Ask students to remain in their groups to complete the 'Let's Do It' worksheet.

4. Report back to the class.

5. Give instructions for habit builder task, 'Alphabet - Objects' (see next page).

Discussion questions

For the Magic Wand:

Did players work together, or by themselves?

What would be the quickest way of getting the magic lantern?

For the Monster:

How did teams work together?

What things helped the team work together?

Did teams get better the longer they played?

ALPHABET - OBJECTS

Form students into teams and tell them about the Alphabet - Objects scavenger hunt where they collect an object beginning with each letter of the alphabet that could be useful for the Party Club celebration after session 9.

Songs, musical instruments, games, masks, decorations, food, clothing, welcome signs, and all sorts of other things might be collected.

The team that collects the most items is the 'Amazing Alphabet Objects' team.

Young People's Pleasant Events

1. Having a bath
2. Collecting things
3. Going on a holiday
4. Watching a favourite TV show
5. Going to the zoo
6. Listening to music
7. Painting
8. Playing with a toy
9. Going to a party
10. Swimming
11. Laughing
12. Learning a joke
13. Practising a magic trick
14. Drawing
15. Playing cards
16. Eating a favourite food
17. Sleeping over at a friend's place
18. Riding a bike
19. Playing a computer game
20. Hobbies
21. Growing a plant or vegetable
22. Looking after a pet
23. Having a friend sleep over
24. Going camping
25. Reading a comic book
26. Flying kites
27. Milking a cow
28. Skateboarding
29. Canoeing
30. Playing music
31. Thinking about your birthday
32. Playing a sport
33. Riding a scooter
34. Talking to your family
35. Roller blading
36. Listening to music
37. Going to scouts or guides
38. Sewing or knitting
39. Singing
40. Playing tennis
41. Collecting shells
42. Gardening
43. Horse riding
44. Having your hair combed
45. Watching fireworks or bonfires
46. Acting
47. Being in a choir
48. Ski-ing
49. Fishing
50. Making a present for someone
51. Photography
52. Being alone
53. Eating chocolate
54. Running barefoot in a park
55. Visiting a playground
56. Playing volleyball
57. Watching or playing football
58. Shopping
59. Going to the museum
60. Remembering good times
61. Opening presents
62. Visiting the aquarium
63. Staying on a farm
64. Talking on the phone
65. Writing a letter
66. Flying in a plane
67. Playing softball
68. Writing a story
69. Jig saw puzzles
70. Ten pin bowling
71. Playing a musical instrument
72. Climbing a tree
73. Surfing a wave
74. Bouncing on a trampoline
75. Cooking
76. Dancing
77. Eating ice-cream
78. Having lunch with a friend
79. Going on a picnic
80. Going to the cinema
81. Passing a test at school
82. Making a new friend
83. Patting a pet
84. Receiving a letter or parcel
85. Having time to do nothing
86. Going out to dinner
87. Painting your face with make-up
88. Making a special effects video

Let's Do It

Some things are best when you do them by yourself,
and other things are better when you do them with a group.

From the list of "Pleasant Events"
find
5 things you prefer to do in a group
and
5 things you prefer to do by yourself

BY MYSELF

1 ....

2 ....

3 ....

4 ....

5 ....

IN A GROUP

1 ....

2 ....

3 ....

4 ....

5 ....

Purpose

THE GREAT SPAGHETTI BOWL of CONNECTIONS

This session helps students to reflect on what friendship means.

Preparation

1. Cut out cards for friendship qualities (see page 37), as well as a 'Most Important' and 'Least Important' sign.

2. Photocopy worksheets, 'Friendship Scenarios' and 'Let's Party', and the habit builder 'The Great Spaghetti Bowl of Connections'.

THE GREAT SPAGHETTI BOWL OF CONNECTIONS cont....

Core Activity

1. Ask students to brainstorm all the qualities of a good friend. (Use 'Words of Friendship' on the next page as a prompt if necessary.)

2. Write each quality on a card until there is one card for each student.

3. Give each student a card each.

4. Ask students to stand in a horse-shoe configuration.

5. At the open end of the horse-shoe place a 'Most Important' sign, while at the other end of the horse shoe place a 'Least Important' sign.

6. Ask the students to consider how important the quality (which is written on their cards) is to being a 'good friend'.

7. In turn, ask each student to place their card along the continuum and to give a reason for where they put it.

8. Instruct students to leave the friendship cards in order on the floor.

9. Ask students to complete the 'Friendship scenarios' worksheet.

10. Return to the continuum and ask if the order of importance changes with each 'Friendship scenario'.

11. Complete the 'Let's Party' worksheet.

12. Ask students to complete their habit builder sheet, 'The Great Spaghetti Bowl of Connections'.

THE GREAT SPAGHETTI BOWL OF CONNECTIONS cont....

Discussion questions

Does everyone want friends? Why are friends important?

Does the order of importance of friendship qualities/characteristics change depending on the situation?

Can you plan to make friends?

What things help you to make friends?

Can people be bad friends?

For 'Let's Party' worksheet:

Is it always possible to include everybody?

What might you do to be sensitive to those who are excluded?

◀◆▶

WORDS of FRIENDSHIP

Kind	Friendly	Happy	Interested
Forgiving	Generous	Supportive	Fun
Reliable	Adventurous	Trustworthy	Loyal
Positive	Energetic	Smart	Tolerant
Understanding	Courageous	Honest	Popular

Friendship Scenarios

Write down the most important quality of a friend in the following situations. If these are difficult to relate to make up your own. They are meant to demonstrate that friendship must survive the bad times, as well as the good times.

You lose your temper and are nasty to your friend.

Most important quality..

You ask if you can copy a friend's homework so you won't get into trouble.

Most important quality..

You are jealous of your friend playing with someone else.

Most important quality..

You forget your lunch.

Most important quality..

Unscramble the sentence to discover the thought from Bunji.
It's never look a by judge Bunji

Let's Party

You are going to have a party! Yes. A fabulous party!

But you have one problem….

You are only allowed to invite six people, but you have eight friends!

WHO WILL YOU CHOOSE?

Adam always invites you to his party.

Sunshine has a health problem and she isn't allowed to get over-excited or to play rough games.

Max is the sort of person who is always the best and who always wins.

Joshua is in a wheel chair and does brilliant wheelies, but you haven't got a disabled toilet.

Gina is funny and people feel happy around her. She is very popular.

Lisa has never been invited to a party. She will be more excited than anyone else to get an invite.

Vu has parents who are very rich. He brings great presents and has promised something extra special for this party.

Madelaine is a good friend who is moving away.

**If you want to discover a thought from Bunji, do this puzzle.
The thought from Bunji is written back to front.**

Traeh a sah enoyreve.

The Great Spaghetti Bowl
of Connections

Draw a great pile of spaghetti with each piece connecting you to
someone you know

IN SEARCH of THE HEART

Purpose

This session helps students to become aware of their different emotions and assists them to label or describe their emotions accurately.

Preparation

Photocopy for all students

'My Favourite Character' worksheet

'My Favourite Character Looks like this.....' worksheet

'Yum & Yuk' habit builder

'Mucking About Map' habit builder.

Core Activity

1.   Begin by pretending to be happy, sad and angry.

2.   Ask the students to guess the emotion.

3.   Call for a volunteer who is prepared to act like an animal.

4.   Privately, instruct the volunteer to act like an angry tiger.

5.   Ask the other students to guess what the volunteer is acting like.

6.   Make a clear space in the room and ask all of the students to circle the space acting out whatever is called: act like a tiger, a tree, a mouse, a footballer, a netballer, a grumpy elephant, a powerful bird, a gigantically, happy dinosaur, a frolicking horse, an angry dog, a scared kitten and a playful penguin.

7.   Brainstorm all the different feelings and make a list.

8.   Introduce the 'My Favourite Character' worksheet.

9.   Distribute habit builder hand outs, 'Yum & Yuk' and 'Mucking about Map'.

Discussion questions

Ask students if they prefer some feelings compared to others?

Do all people prefer the same feelings?

For My Favourite Character worksheet:

Think of your favourite movie or book.

Who is your favourite character in the movie or the book?

What is your favourite character like?

What are the most common emotions your favourite character demonstrates?

My Favourite Character

My favourite movie or book is

. . . .

. . . .

. . . .

My favourite character in that book or movie is?

. . . .

. . . .

I like it because

. . . .

. . . .

. . . .

. . . .

The best way to describe my favourite character is

. . . .

. . . .

. . . .

. . . .

Unjumble the words to discover the thought from Bunji.

Wnok ahwt oyu tnaw.

K- - - W- - - Y- - W- - -.

My Favourite Character Looks Like This.......

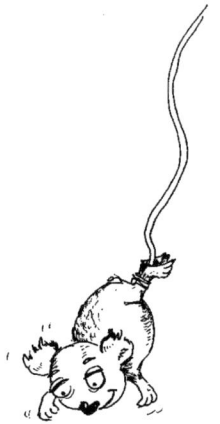

Draw a picture of your favourite character

Yum & Yuk

Make a list of 5 things that make you feel bad (yuk) and 5 things that make you feel good (yum).

Yum	Yuk

Yum

1..

2..

3..

4..

5..

Yuk

1..

2..

3..

4..

5..

Mucking About Map

Choose a place where you have fun or muck around (it could be home, school, the park, the beach or the whole neighbourhood).

DRAW A MAP OF IT

Mucking About Map

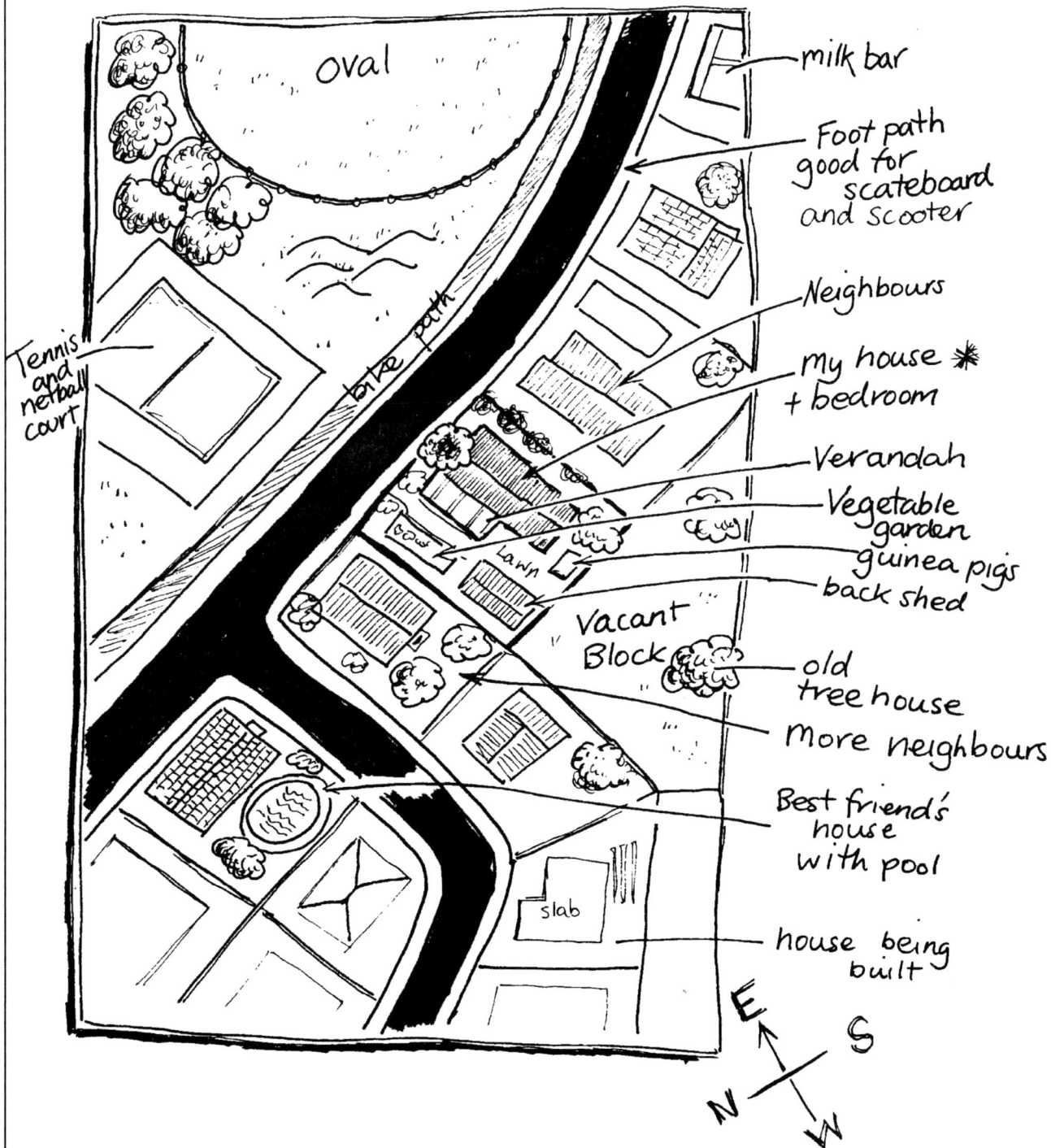

oval

milk bar

Foot path good for scateboard and scooter

Neighbours

my house ✳ + bedroom

Verandah

Vegetable garden

guinea pigs

back shed

bike path

Tennis and netball court

Vacant Block

old tree house

More neighbours

Best friend's house with pool

slab

house being built

cow

Lawn

The Feelings Barometer

Purpose

This session helps students to become aware of their different emotions and how emotions are influenced by their senses.

Preparation

1. Photocopy the "My Personal Shield" worksheets & the "Yum & Yuk" habit builder .

2. Materials needed for the 'Feelings Barometer': cardboard; scissors; studs (if available). Sensation objects that provide a variety of touch, taste and smell sensations such as an onion, mud, lemonade, sandpaper, fur, gooey play dough, an orange, a biscuit and a wet soggy sponge.

3. Materials to make a personal shield (optional).

Core Activity

1. On a large piece of paper or cardboard, make a 'feelings' barometer for the class. Additionally, if you wish you could ask each student to make their own 'Feelings Barometer'.

The Feelings Barometer

1. The 'Feelings Barometer' could be pinned to the wall or put on each student's desk.

2. Lay out one of the sensation objects at a time. Conceal the object from the students, either by having them stand in a line outside the room, by using blindfolds, by using a screen, or by placing the sensation objects in a box that obscures them from view. Ask students in turn to touch, taste or smell as appropriate. Once a student has had their turn, they should write down the sensation object and the feeling it gave them.

3. Rate the intensity of the feeling on the 'Feelings barometer'.

4. Show some paintings and ask students how it makes them feel, or play different pieces of music and once again explore the range of emotions being expressed.

5. Create a Personal Shield (using the worksheet) or alternately, students could make a Personal Shield from cardboard using the information from the worksheets, and placing the strengths and feelings they want to show the world on the front of the shield, and the words of encouragement and the personal motto on the inside of the shield.

6. Distribute the 'Yum and Yuk' habit builder.

Discussion questions

Which feelings do you like?

What are some ways you might influence your feelings?

Do people always influence their feelings in a good way?

How do other people influence your feelings?

My Personal Shield

Unjumble the words, and it is a big jumble,
to discover the thought from Bunji.

Kpee Lkngioo

K - - - L - - - - - -

My Personal Shield

Is your personal shield something you would wear on your jacket, or a big solid shield that could be used to defend yourself against spears?

On one side put the strengths and feelings you want to show to the world.

On the other side think of a motto, or words that will give you encouragement.

My Feelings	My Motto
1	1 ....
....	....
2	2 ....
....	....
3	3 ....
....	....

Yum

A thing that made me feel good each day is...

DAY ONE:

DAY TWO:

DAY THREE:

DAY FOUR:

DAY FIVE:

DAY SIX:

DAY SEVEN:

FROM YUK TO YUM

Purpose

This session helps students to become aware of their different emotions and how emotions are influenced by the things they do.

Preparation

1. Photocopy the 'Pleasant Events' handout, the 'My Favourite Thing' worksheet and the 'These are a few of my favourite things....' habit builder for each student.

Core Activity

1. Distribute copies of the 'Pleasant Events' handout.

2. Ask students to tick those activities they would enjoy.

3. Add other things students enjoy that are not on the list.

4. Prepare 'My Favourite Thing' worksheet and have each student give a presentation to the class.

5. Habit builder: Select one (different) activity from the 'Pleasant Events' handout to do each day for one week.

Discussion questions

Do you enjoy a lot of things or only a few things?

How do you tell if you enjoy something?

Does everybody have the same reasons why they enjoy things?

Young People's Pleasant Events

1. Having a bath
2. Collecting things
3. Going on a holiday
4. Watching a favourite TV show
5. Going to the zoo
6. Listening to music
7. Painting
8. Playing with a toy
9. Going to a party
10. Swimming
11. Laughing
12. Learning a joke
13. Practising a magic trick
14. Drawing
15. Playing cards
16. Eating a favourite food
17. Sleeping over at a friends place
18. Riding a bike
19. Playing a computer game
20. Hobbies
21. Growing a plant or vegetable
22. Looking after a pet
23. Having a friend sleep over
24. Going camping
25. Reading a comic book
26. Flying kites
27. Milking a cow
28. Skateboarding
29. Canoeing
30. Playing music
31. Thinking about your birthday
32. Playing a sport
33. Riding a scooter
34. Talking to your family
35. Roller blading
36. Listening to music
37. Going to scouts or guides
38. Sewing or knitting
39. Singing
40. Playing tennis
41. Collecting shells
42. Gardening
43. Horse riding
44. Having your hair combed
45. Watching fireworks or bonfires
46. Acting
47. Being in a choir
48. Ski-ing
49. Fishing
50. Making a present for someone
51. Photography
52. Being alone
53. Eating chocolate
54. Running barefoot in a park
55. Visiting a playground
56. Playing volleyball
57. Watching or playing football
58. Shopping
59. Going to the museum
60. Remembering good times
61. Opening presents
62. Visiting the aquarium
63. Staying on a farm
64. Talking on the phone
65. Writing a letter
66. Flying in a plane
67. Playing softball
68. Writing a story
69. Jig saw puzzles
70. Ten pin bowling
71. Playing a musical instrument
72. Climbing a tree
73. Surfing a wave
74. Bouncing on a trampoline
75. Cooking
76. Dancing
77. Eating ice-cream
78. Having lunch with a friend
79. Going on a picnic
80. Going to the cinema
81. Passing a test at school
82. Making a new friend
83. Patting a pet
84. Receiving a letter or parcel
85. Having time to do nothing
86. Going out to dinner
87. Painting your face with make-up
88. Making a special effects video

My Favourite Thing

Prepare a talk or demonstration for the class where you describe one of your favourite things.

One of my favourite things is

....

....

I am enjoying my favourite things best when

....

....

....

My favourite thing can make me feel like

....

....

....

On the 'Feelings Barometer' I would score my favourite thing at

....

To discover the thought from Bunji, write the following words backwards and then unscramble the sentence.

Semit hsirehc doog eht.

These are a few of my favourite things

Day	Thing I Did	How Much I Enjoyed It

Masters of the HEART

Purpose

This session teaches students to read the non-verbal cues from others, which is a vital skill for emotional intelligence.

Preparation

Photocopy the 'Feeling Faces' worksheet and 'An Interview with my Parent' habit builder. Prepare 'Feelings Cards' (see page 62) and locate a roll of sticky labels.

Core Activity

1. **Play the Sticky Labels Feelings Game.**

   ➤ Transcribe the feelings from the Feelings Cards worksheet on to sticky labels.

   ➤ Form students into teams.

   ➤ Place a sticky label on a student's forehead.

   ➤ The aim of the game is for the student to guess the feeling on their forehead.

   ➤ They may ask questions and the other members of the team can nod or shake their heads but they cannot speak.

   ➤ The other members of the team can also give hints without speaking. For example, if the feeling is sad, a student might pretend to be crying, or the other members of the team might treat the member as if they are sad.

2. Use a piece of dialogue from 'The Dialogue for Theatre Sports Sheet'.

   ➤ Have two readers select feeling cards without showing them to the others and read through the dialogue using the feeling they have chosen.

   ➤ After each reading, the other students try to guess the emotions expressed.

3. Ask students to draw a picture expressing some of the feelings described on the 'Feelings Cards'.

4. Habit Builders: Students to interview their parent or guardians regarding using 'An Interview with My Parent/ Guardian Sheet'.

Discussion questions

Using a prop like a collection of a series of photos and art, pictures or magazine cuttings of peoples faces:

➤ Ask students to try to work out the feelings being expressed.

➤ Ask students to explain how they worked out the feelings expressed.

➤ Make a list of all the feelings which students can imagine.

➤ Is it possible to pick how people are feeling by the way they say things?

➤ What other ways help you read a person's feelings?

Dialogue for Theatre Sports

Script One

Student A: How are you today?

Student B: I think I'm very well, thankyou.

Student A: That's good, I went to the beach on the weekend.

Student B: I went to see a movie with my family.

Student A: That must have been good.

Student B: See you later.

Student A: Goodbye.

Script Two

Student A: Pass the salt please.

Student B: OK, could you pass me a glass so I can have a drink?

Student A: Of course, I'd be delighted.

Student B: Now please pass me a plate.

Student A: Can't you reach it?

Student B: No, my bottom is glued to my chair.

Script Three

Student A: Would you like to come to my party?

Student B: When is it?

Student A: Next Saturday, there will be some great food.

Student B: Are other people coming?

Student A: I hope so, I haven't asked them yet.

Student B: Are you sure you want me to come to your party?

Student A: Well, you are supposed to be my closest friend.

Feelings Cards

Happy	Excited	Annoyed	Delighted
Worried	Polite	Irritated	Friendly
Funny	Fearful	Amused	Kind
Interested	Bored	Tired	Lively
Relieved	Thirsty	Hungry	Want to be Alone
Quiet	Laughing	Scared	Curious

Heart Masters Extra Activities

Using face paint, students draw emotions on their faces. The other students have to guess the emotion.

Ask others what makes them feel good - develop a survey of staff/ students and /or parents.

Valentine's Day - save the Valentine's Day entries in the local paper - scan the paper to ensure that every class member's name is mentioned. Photocopy and ask students to cut out those entries that use their name.

The Thank You Chair - one student sits in the 'Thank You Chair' while the other class members in turn say one positive thing to them. The student in the chair can only say, "thank you".

Charades - act out a feeling. Students have to guess. Fear, Happy, Sad, Angry, Frustrated, Excited, Powerless, Content.

Use a piece of writing or a poem. In pairs, distribute feelings cards. Read out the poem several times with different emotional tones, Ask students to select a feeling card that best describes the way you have read the poem.

Puppets of Feelings: in teams build a series of large, paper mache puppets. Each puppet characterises a feeling- angry, happy, sad, and unsure. If there are more teams add other feelings - worried, excited, and content. Names can be given to the puppets - eg. Sad Cyril, Angry Agatha, Unsure Ursula and Happy Hercules.

Create a human sculpture with other students to express a feeling. See if others can guess.

Feeling Faces

HAPPY   SAD   ANGRY!

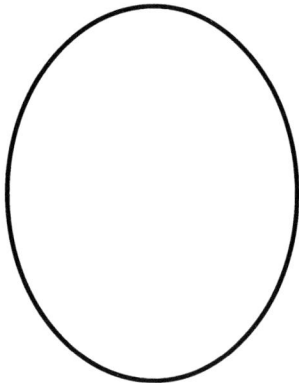   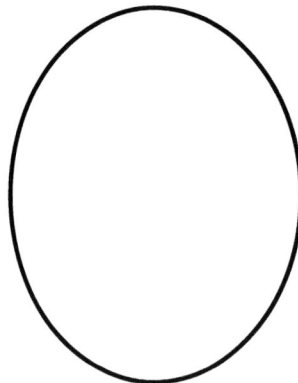   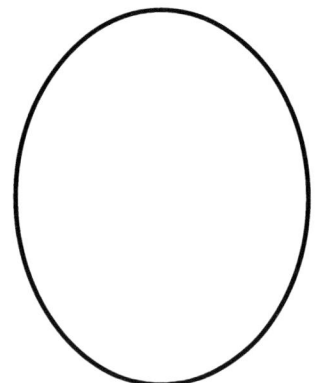

WORRIED   EXCITED   FEARFUL

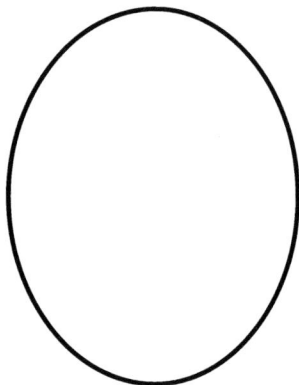   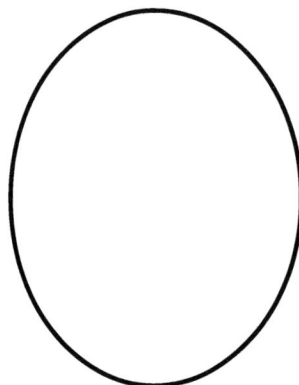   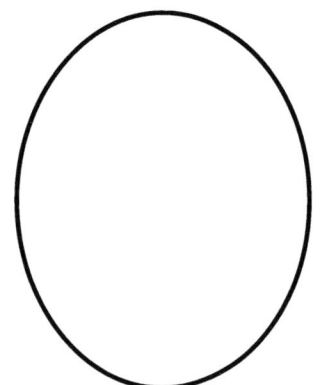

Draw a face to show the feeling above each circle.

To discover the thought from Bunji, unscramble the words. Hint: the second word begins with 'f'.
Adb ngfesile saps
B - - F - - - - - - - P - - -

An Interview with my Parent/Guardian

What things made you feel happy when you were in primary school?

What things made you feel sad when you were in primary school?

Do these things still make you feel like you did then?

What is one of your happiest memories from when you were young?

What do you do to make yourself happy now?

Favourite Feelings

Think of one of your favourite feelings.

When do you often have this feeling?

Are there things you can do to create this feeling?

What could you do in the mornings to make a positive start to each day?

THE PARTY CLUB - CELEBRATING

Purpose

Organise a party to practise the skills students have learned, as well as to celebrate.

Warning

This activity could result in fun.

Core Activity

1.	Break students into groups and allocate tasks.

2.	One group is to survey everybody about their favourite 'feel good' party foods, to design a list of 'feel good' food and drinks.

3.	Another group is to survey students about their favourite games and to organise a 'fun and fantastic' games time table for the party. (Tip: Make sure all of the games are ready the day before.)

4.	One group is to design 'friendly' invitations and send them out to all the students in the class. Everybody must be invited.

5.	One group is to make party decorations and 'feel good' signs for the party.

6.	Each student could bring one piece of their favourite party music.

———————⟨◆⟩———————

Discussion questions

Discuss the creation of a party club.

What makes a great party?

How did you feel?

How did other people feel during the party?

NB: This activity could occur at any point during the programme.

———————⟨◆⟩———————

ENERGISERS!

Purpose

To explore how to help build positive feelings.

Note: This session could be integrated into the Party Club session.

We all need to be a 'great friend' to ourselves before we can be a 'great friend' to others. Part of being a 'great friend' to ourselves is not only looking after our minds and bodies, but also giving ourselves energy.

We all need Energisation!

The more energy we have the more resilient we are. To squeeze life for everything it has to offer, we need energy. And what gives us energy?

Preparation

1. Be positive

2. Photocopy 'Energising the Senses' worksheet and 'Favourite Feelings' habit builder.

Core Activity

1. Ask students or groups of students to choose one of the following activities and present it to the class in the following session.

2. When presenting their 'feel good' food, costume, pleasant event or bedroom, they should explain why it makes them 'feel good'.

3. As a class, make a list of things that will help create a classroom where everybody feels positive. (You can add to this list in the future.)

4. Complete the worksheets 'Energising the Senses'and the habit builder 'Favourite Things'.

Eating for Health

Groups of students could make a menu for a high energy, healthy and scrumptious lunch. Ask each student to think of a food that makes them feel energised after eating it.

Or

Dressing up

How do clothes make us feel? Would you wear your school uniform to a party? Or your bikini or your speedos to an English class? Clothes say things about us. The colours we wear, the style, the fit, the materials we choose, the labels we buy. Bring the most outrageous dress ups you can find and have a fashion parade.

Or

Enjoying yourself for Health

Plan a great day out that is fun, healthy and energising. Refer to your list of 'Young People's Pleasant Events' for ideas.

Or

The World's Greatest Bedroom

Design a bedroom that is perfect for the everyday highly energised switched off young people.

If you get really carried away, you might like to make some improvements to energise the

classroom. At least make some suggestions anyway.

Discussion questions

What makes you feel good?

Can you influence your feelings?

How are feelings created?

Are some feelings a habit?

◀◆▶

Energising the Senses

To discover the thought from Bunji, complete the idea:

Do your (opposite of 'worst').

Energising the Senses

What sounds make you feel good?

Running water...   Farm animals...   Music...   Birds...
Wind in the trees...   Possums on the roof...   Flushing toilets

....

....

....

Does anything make you feel different by looking at it?

Nice clothes...   A tidy room...   A car accident...   A pelican flying past...

....

....

....

What is the nicest thing you have ever touched?

Have you ever put your hand down in the dark and touched something that moves?

How about picking up rotting rubbish after the cat has taken it from the bin?

Or something nice, like a new silk dress, or a new basketball, or a baby's cheek

....

....

....

What are your favourite smells?

Exhaust from cars...   Fresh flowers...   Aromatherapy potions...
The breeze off the ocean...   Rotting meat full of maggots... Smelly socks...

....

....

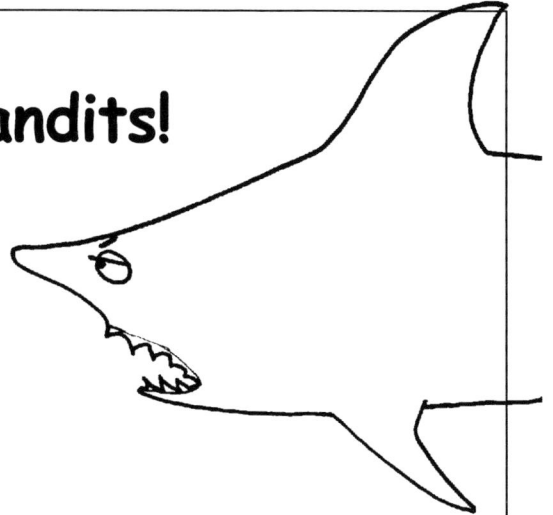

Session ELEVEN

Life Bandits!

Purpose

To build awareness of negative influences; the things that steal energy

Preparation

1. Provide a dice for each group.
2. Photocopy the 'Dicing with The Life Bandits' game.
3. Photocopy 'The Life Bandits' worksheet.

Core Activities

1. Distribute the 'Dicing with The Life Bandits' game to students along with a dice per game (if you don't have enough dice, students can share).

2. Explain that students should roll the dice once for each category to develop a word picture of an imaginary person by circling the squares according to the number on the dice. For example, if a student throws a 3 for 'habit', their imaginary person 'plays a lot of sport'. If they then throw a 1 for personality, their imaginary person is 'argumentative'. If they then throw a 4 for 'talent' their person has a talent for learning, and if they throw a 2 on their fourth throw they are a good best friend.

3. Answer the questions on the 'Dice with The Life Bandits' sheet.

4. Ask students to present their characters to the class, keeping in mind discussion questions where appropriate.

5. Students can commence their worksheet.

Discussion Points

How often do you plan things to energise yourself?

What things sap your energy?

Are you often low on energy?

Dicing with the Life Bandits

NUMBER Habit	1	2	3	4	5	6
	ONLY EATS JUNK FOOD	WATCHES 5 HOURS TELEVISION EACH DAY	PLAYS A LOT OF SPORT	LOVES SINGING AND DANCING ENJOYS A LOT OF ACTIVITIES	EATS A BALANCED DIET AND	READS BOOKS ALL OF THE TIME
Personality	ARGUMENT-ATIVE	GIVES COMPLIMENTS	FRIENDLY	SEES THE GOOD SIDE OF PEOPLE	ROUGH	WORRIES A LOT
Talent	TALKING	LISTENING	SPORT	LEARNING	SLEEPING	AVOIDING
Other Influences	BOSSY PARENTS	A GOOD BEST FRIEND	A BIG FAMILY	OFTEN LEFT ALONE	LOVES SCHOOL	DISLIKES TEACHER

QUESTIONS

1. Describe what the person is like.
2. What things help them to feel positive?
3. What things steal their energy?
4. What might they do to protect their feelings?

THE HEART MASTERS   76

Life Bandits

How you feel inside is as important as what is going on outside. For example, you might be at a party but you still don't feel really good. You can have all the nicest things in the world, you can have anything you want, but if you don't stop to enjoy things, if you don't listen to the nice sounds, see the incredible sights, lay a hand on the tantalising touches, taste the delicious foods and smell the wonderful smells, you will miss out. And one day you might even start to think that the good feelings in life have been stolen from you. You risk becoming a bit likc a sack of spuds, so to speak.

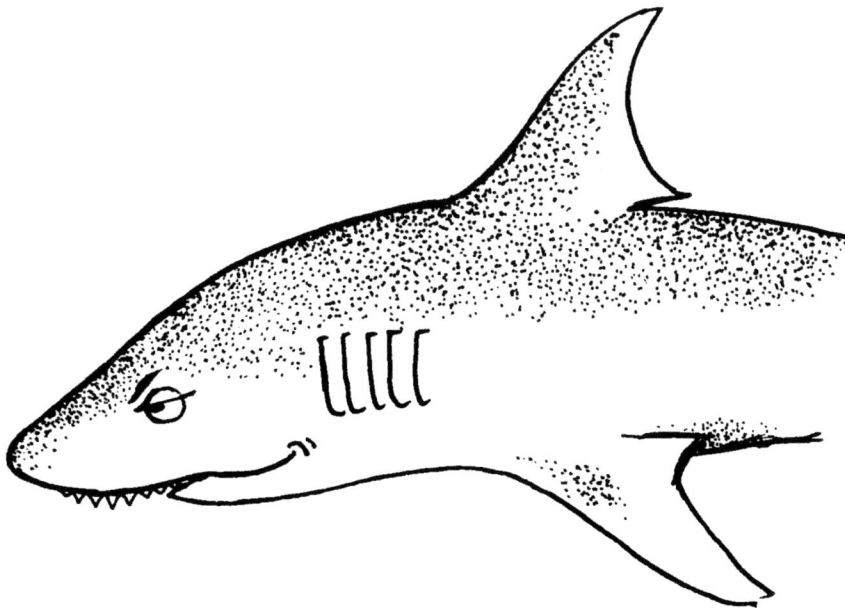

Life Bandits

<u>Rate from 1 – 10 the biggest life bandits;</u>
<u>1</u> being the biggest life bandit and <u>10</u> being the least powerful life bandit.

Life Bandits.....

Poor sleep	....
Anger	....
Being perfect	....
Big meals	....
Wasting time	....
Loud noise	....
Grumpy teachers	....
Homework	....
Tidying bedrooms	....
Stress	....

To discover the thought from Bunji, join the correct endings to the words:
nd, augh, ing, ance.

S _ _ _ , d _ _ _ _ _ , a _ _ , l _ _ _ _ , but no kissing!

PRICKLY PROBLEMS

Purpose

To explore ways of coping with problems.

Preparation

1.   Make 'Action' cards (see page 81).

2.   Photocopy, 'Personal Problems' worksheet.

Note: Students should not be compelled to do the problem solving activity. They may watch the others if they prefer. Students should only write things they are prepared to share with the class. Teachers should also talk to students about being trustworthy and confidential. If a student is saying something to their detriment, or to someone else's detriment, the teacher may sensitively interrupt and talk to the student later.

Core Activity

1. Ask students to think of something that has recently caused them stress or made them upset.

2. Ask them to write what happened and how they felt.

3. Then put stressful incidents into a box and ask students to choose one from somebody else. If they pick up their own, they return it to the box and choose another.

4. Make action cards from the following list. (If cards are not possible, teachers could write 2 columns on the blackboard or overhead projector.)

5. Spread the action cards on the floor, and ask one student at a time to stand up and choose the card that describes what they did when they were stressed.

6. Discuss how this helped or made things worse.

7. Ask students:

   ➤ Did this action help relieve your stress or make it worse?

   ➤ Would another problem solving card be more helpful?

8. Complete worksheet.

9. Ask students to talk to their parents or another trusted person about:

   ➤ when they should share their problems

   ➤ with who they should share their problems.

———————— ❮◆❯ ————————

Discussion questions

Do all people have problems?

Does everybody cope with problems in the same way?

Are some problems worse than others?

When should you seek help with problems?

PRICKLY PROBLEMS cont....

ACTION CARDS

I MAKE A JOKE	I THINK ABOUT MY GOOD POINTS
I MAKE A PLAN OF WHAT TO DO	I START DOING THINGS, ANYTHING
I TRY TO REASON WITH THE PERSON CAUSING THE PROBLEM	I ACCEPT THAT I PROBABLY CAUSED THE PROBLEM
I KEEP THINGS TO MYSELF	I SAY ROTTEN THINGS TO MYSELF
I GET HOT, BREATHE FAST AND SCREW MY FACE UP	I THINK ABOUT IT ALL THE TIME
I TALK TO NO-ONE	I IGNORE IT
I PLAY SPORT	I HIT MY LITTLE SISTER OR BROTHER
I YELL AT MY MUM OR DAD	I TALK TO SOMEONE ABOUT IT
I THINK ABOUT HOW I MIGHT HELP OTHERS	I EXERCISE AND SLEEP A LOT
I TRY TO RELAX	I DON"T FEEL LIKE EATING
I EAT LOLLIES	I GET SCARED
I STOP MYSELF FROM WORRYING	I TALK TO MY PARENTS OR AN ADULT
I TALK TO A FRIEND	I CRY A LOT

PRICKLY PROBLEMS cont....

Letter to Parents.

Dear Parent,

In class we are talking about problem solving. We have asked your child to discuss problem solving with you.

An important part of learning to be a good problem solver occurs by knowing when to seek help or advice.

Different people are good at giving different advice. Parents or close and trusted adult friends are often an appropriate starting point. They might be all the help that is needed. But sometimes other help is needed. For example, if it is a problem at school, a student might need to talk to a teacher.

It is also helpful for young people to discuss the sorts of people that may give wrong or misleading advice. For example, a friend might be good to ask about the best football boots, dancing shoes or nail polish. But they may not be the most appropriate person to help with a health problem.

Considerations like trustworthiness, kindness and expertise are all important considerations when deciding with whom to share a problem.

We encourage you to discuss these issues with your child.

If you would like further information, please contact me on

....

Yours sincerely,

Personal Problems

Make a list of the people you can talk to when you have a problem.

Next to their name, explain the type of problem you would talk to them about.

Example.

Person	Problem	Reason
Parent	Most problems	They love me and I trust them
Doctor	Health problems	They know about health
....	....	....

How can talking to someone help with problems?

....

....

Why wouldn't you tell some people about your problems?

....

....

Solve the riddles to discover the thought from Bunji.

Hint: a few	_ O _ E
Hint: sunrise to sunset	_ _ Y _
Hint: a bouncy thing	B _ _ J _ S
Hint: opposite of 'do' (2 words)	_ O _ O _
Hint: up and down	_ _ U N C _

DOLPHIN POWER

Purpose

This session helps students learn that different thoughts can lead to different feelings. The previous session focused on external things making young people feel good or bad. This session aims to give students some of the skills to develop internal strategies for feeling good.

Preparation

Photocopy for the class, 'Dolphins and Sharks,' 'Happy and Sad Thoughts' worksheets, and 'The Dolphin and Shark Thoughts Collection' habit builder.

Core Activity

1. Ask students to close their eyes.

2. Ask students to notice what they think and feel as you read a 'neutral thought' from the 'Feelings and Thoughts' sheet on the next page.

3. After each thought ask students:

    ➢ What did you think?

    ➢ How did you feel?

4. Ask enough students to get a diverse range of thoughts and feelings.

5. Then ask students to close their eyes again. Now add to the original thought by reading the embellishment (see page 59). Ask students if their feelings have changed?

6. Continue this process until students begin to understand the relationship between their thoughts and their feelings.

7. Ask students to complete the 'Happy and Sad Thoughts' worksheet, and the 'Dolphins and Sharks' worksheet.

8. Distribute habit builder hand out and explain to students how to complete it over the proceeding week.

———————————⟨◆⟩———————————

Discussion questions

How do happy thoughts make you feel?

What is a happy thought?

How do sad thoughts make you feel?

What is a sad thought?

Do your thoughts influence your feelings?

Feelings and Thoughts Sheet

Neutral thought: **Bedtime**

Embellishment: It is a cold and windy night and you are snuggled up in a warm and cosy bed.

Neutral thought: **Holidays**

Embellishment: While you are away you will miss your best friend's birthday party.

Neutral thought: **Losing a tooth**

Embellishment: You are going to get money from the tooth fairy.

Neutral thought: **Moving to a new city**

Embellishment: It's an exciting adventure and anything could happen.

Neutral thought: **Going to a new school**

Embellishment: You will stay in touch with your old friends and have a chance to meet a whole lot of new ones.

Neutral thought: **Going on a school camp**

Embellishment: The food will be disgusting.

Dolphins and Sharks

In this book, we represent happy or good thoughts as dolphins and sad, angry or frightened thoughts as sharks. If you don't like these labels you can change them to something that suits you.

SCHOOL

Dolphin thought ....

....

Shark thought ....

....

HOLIDAY

Dolphin thought ....

....

Shark thought: ....

....

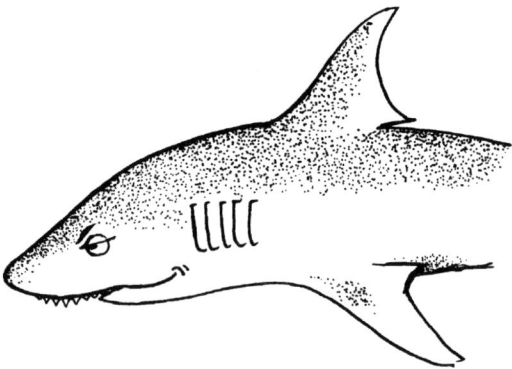

PARTY

Dolphin thought ....

....

Shark thought: ....

....

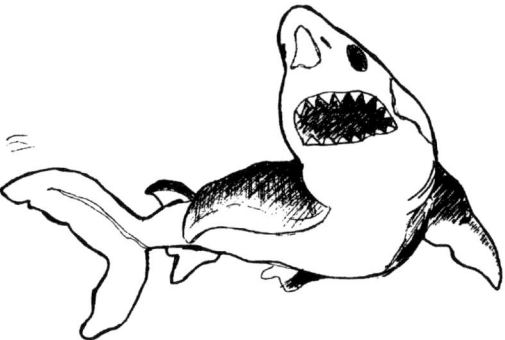

Happy and Sad

Imagine a dolphin among a pod jumping in and out of the water.

How do you feel?

....

....

Now, imagine a shark prowling a seal colony about to chase a playful little pup.

How do you feel?

....

....

Happy and Sad

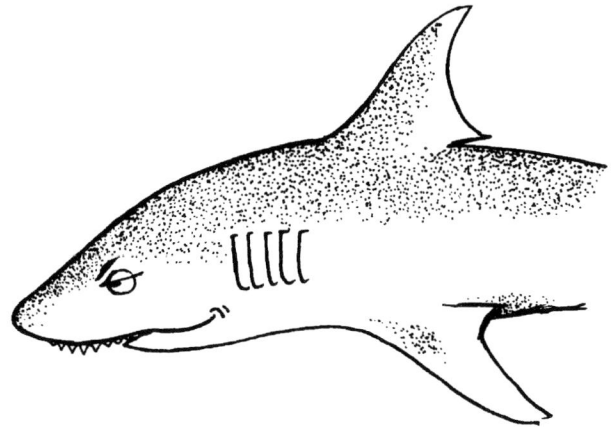

Draw a face to show your feelings about the dolphin and the shark.

DOLPHIN

SHARK

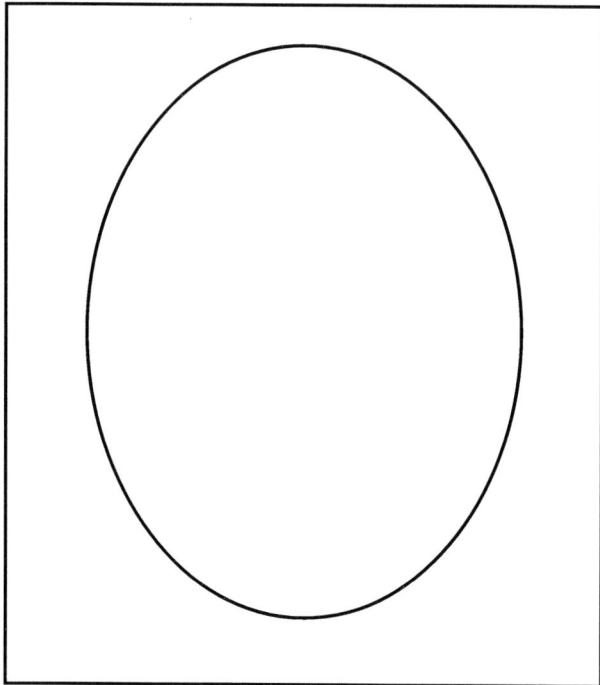

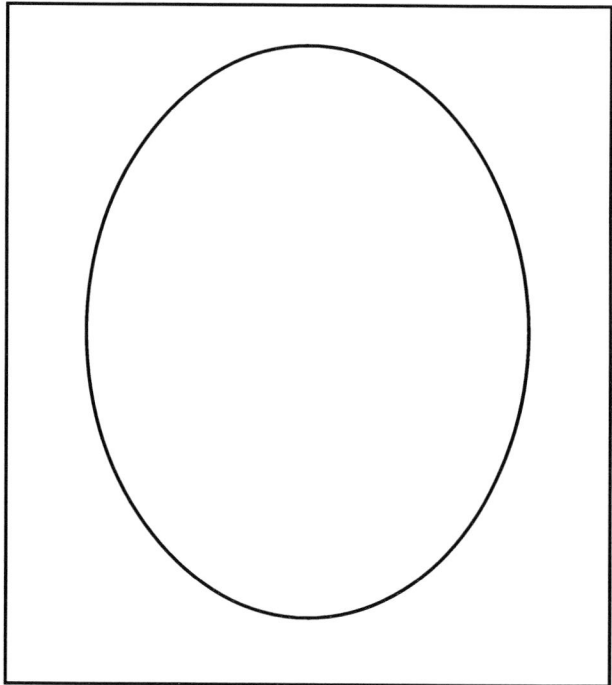

Unjumble the sentence to discover the thought from Bunji.
There is every solution problem for a.

The Dolphins and Sharks Thoughts Collection

Make a list of 5 dolphin and 5 shark thoughts that come into your mind over a week.

Dolphins

1 ....
2 ....
3 ....
4 ....
5 ....

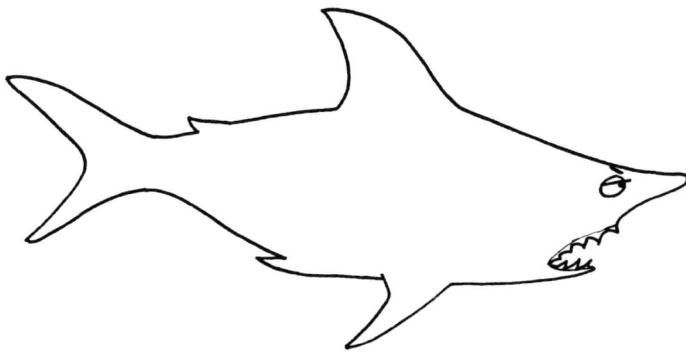

Sharks

1 ....
2 ....
3 ....
4 ....
5 ....

THE MAZE

Purpose

This session helps students learn that different comments can lead to different feelings. This session encourages students to make encouraging and positive comments, rather than negative and discouraging comments.

Preparation

1.   Photocopy a class set of the 'The Underwater Maze' worksheet.

Core Activity

1. Form students into groups of 6 or so.

2. Each group forms a circle

3. Ask students to raise their left hands and join them with a person opposite..

3. Ask students to raise their left hands and join them with a person opposite. Then raise their right hands and join with somebody else.

4. Once everybody has joined hands, tell them to untangle the knot without letting go of anybody's hand. (However, students can re-position their hands if their arm is being twisted.)

5. The team that untangles itself, and is standing holding hands in a circle first is the winner.

6. Write two columns on the board: dolphin (positive) and shark (negative).

7. Ask students to think back to the game and to list the dolphin and shark comments made by other students during the activity.

8. As a class using the negative comments, think of how they could be changed into positive comments.

9. On a larger piece of paper or cardboard draw the outline of a dolphin and a shark. Pin them on the board and each time the teacher or students notice a negative or positive comment, they should write it onto the sheet. At the end of the week, see whether the shark or the dolphin has the most comments.

10. Do the 'Underwater Maze' worksheet.

11. This could be continued over a number of weeks to see how far down the class can get the shark thoughts and how high the class can get the dolphin thoughts. Perhaps a set target, and have a celebration when the target is achieved.

NB: A range of team games can be used for this activity.

◆

Discussion questions

How do shark comments make you feel?

How do dolphin comments make you feel?

Which comments made you try harder?

Which ones made you feel less enthusiastic?

Why do people make shark comments?

◆

Dolphin Power

Ask students to select a member of their family to surprise by making outstanding exceptional, mind-blistering amazing comments this week.

The Underwater Maze

Find the cross and colour it in. Now from there you begin. You have 3 minutes of air. Concentrate, persevere, be positive, and you will escape and swim away.

Cool Compliments

Purpose

This session helps students to think and say supportive comments. If students are in the habit of being positive towards other people, they are more capable of being positive and supportive to themselves.

Preparation

Photocopy a class set of the 'Cool Compliments' worksheet.

Core Activity

1.   Explain to students that they must be positive in this activity.

2.   Ask for a volunteer who is to leave the class (the receiver).

3.   Instruct the other students to list three things they like or respect about the absent student. Write the 3 comments on a note to give them.

4.   Ask for a volunteer to give (the giver) the three compliments when the student returns.

5.   When the receiver returns to class, the giver stands straight and gives the three class compliments while looking the receiver in the eye.

6.   Repeat the process for all students who wish to participate.

7.   Alternately, you could use the "Thank You" chair activity outlined in the Heart Masters Extension Activities.

8.   Complete the 'Cool Compliments' worksheet.

9.   Explain the 'Invisible Amigos' activity and draw names from a hat.

―――――――――――――<◆>―――――――――――――

Discussion questions

Is it difficult to give compliments?

How does it feel to receive compliments?

Do students often give themselves compliments?

Invisible Amigos

Write all students' names on separate pieces of paper and put them into a container.

Each student is to draw out a name.

If a student draws their own name, they should replace it and draw another.

For the following week, you should be a good friend to the person without telling them.

At the end of the week, each student should try to work out who was their good friend for the week and explain how they knew.

Cool Compliments

Unjumble the words to discover the thought from Bunji.
Eb lcen !

Cool Compliments

Who was the last person you gave a compliment to outside of class?

Who was the last person who gave you a compliment?

What was the compliment?

Do you ever give yourself compliments?

Give yourself three compliments.

THE PEACE MAKERS

Purpose

To enable students to identify 'angry' feelings

To allow students to learn the cues for their own anger.

Preparation

1.   Photocopy the 'Crazy Cartoon' worksheets.

Core Activity

Instructional note: The lists students make from the activities below can be used during the following sessions. They are to demonstrate how the body reacts to feelings or thoughts. When you become angry your body speeds up, when you are calm your body works more slowly and peacefully, and then again, sometimes you can't see things clearly, almost like you are dizzy. When your judgement is impaired, it is hard to make good decisions.

1. Ask students to stand in front of a step.

2. Instruct students to step up and down until they are panting and their heart rates have increased.

3. Ask students to lie on their backs, close their eyes and to breathe deeply. Try to only think about their breathing.

4. Ask for a volunteer and spin them around until they are a bit dizzy. When the spinning finishes, ask students to walk in a straight line.

5. Draw three columns on the board. Ask students to describe what happened to their bodies, as well as how they felt, for each activity.

6. Then label the columns, anger (for the step activity), calming down (for the meditative activity) and perspective (for the spinning activity).

7. Ask the students to copy the lists into their work books.

8. Ask students if they would add anything else to the anger column.

9. Ask students to collect photos of people with angry faces.

10. Distribute 'Crazy Cartoons' worksheet and explain how to complete it.

Discussion questions

How do you know when you are angry?

Where do you first feel your anger?

What is the first thing somebody would notice when you get angry?

How can you tell when other people are angry?

I'm Angry!

Ask students to talk to their parents about:

How they tell when their children are angry?

How do they help them calm down?

At what times are their children most likely to get angry?

Crazy Cartoons

Answer the equations and put the words in their places to discover the thought from Bunji

Meaning (2x3) = 6

Have   (1+8-5)

Can   (9-6)

Word   (21-12)

Than   (3+4)

A   (1,000,000/1,000,000)

A   (8/1)

More   (1+1-6+9)

Look   (0+2)

1 .... 2........... 3 ....

4 .... 5........... 6 Meaning

7 .... 8........... 9 ....

Crazy Cartoons

Create words to go with the cartoons.

Session SEVENTEEN

WHAT CHEEZES ME OFF!

Purpose

To learn how to read the anger of other people.

To make a plan of how to calm down when angry.

Preparation

1. Photocopy 'Calm and in Control' worksheet and 'Would You Believe It' habit builder for each student.

Core Activity

1. Each student takes turns in standing in the front of the class and explaining what makes them angry (what cheezes me off!)

2. Then ask them to show how they act when they are angry.

3. The other class members observe how you can tell that the person is angry.

4. The class join together in an empathic scream - 'CHEEZZZZZ".

5. Play the 'Common Chaos' game with an added twist.

    ➤ Arrange enough seats for every student in a circle, less one.

    ➤ Ask for a volunteer. Everybody else sits in a circle. The volunteer thinks of a common characteristic and calls it out. All those students to whom it applies jump up out of their seat and run to another seat on the other side of the circle. The last person standing goes into the middle and calls out another characteristic.

    ➤ Some examples are:

        a. Everybody who likes ice cream.

        b. All of the boys or girls.

        c. Everybody who plays sport.

        d. Everybody who is smiling.

        e. Everybody who had toast for breakfast.

        f. Everybody who watched television last night.

    ➤ Once students understand the game, add another element. When you blow the whistle they must freeze immediately.

    ➤ The last person to freeze goes into the middle.

        Distribute worksheet 'Calm and In Control' and explain to students how to complete it.

        Distribute habit builder hand out, 'Would You Believe It?', and ask students to explain what they would do?

‹◆›

Discussion questions

For empathic scream activity:

How can you tell when other people are angry?

Do all people show their anger in the same ways?

For Game Activity

Why is it difficult to stop suddenly?

Do some people find it easier than others?

Can you stop yourself from getting angry?

How might you calm yourself down when you are angry?

(add to the calming down list from the previous lesson.)

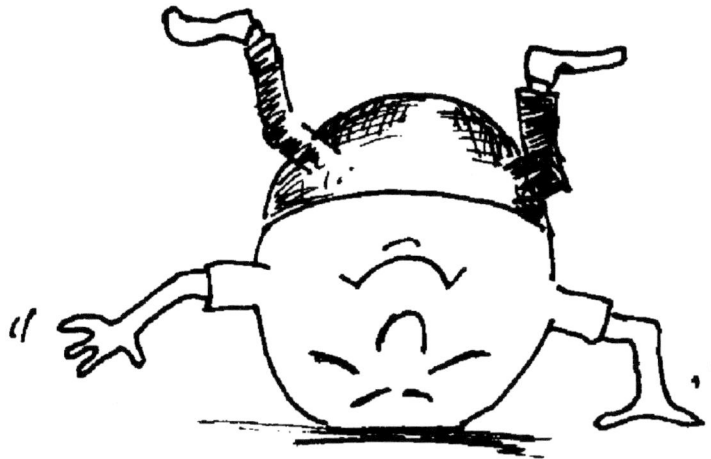

Calm and in Control

| Angry Person | Calm Person |

Explain how you can go from being an angry person to being a calm person.

....

....

Explain how you can stop yourself from being angry by

....

....

Explain how you can calm yourself down by

....

....

To discover the thought from Bunji fill in the vowels
S _ LF C _ NTR _ L T _ K _ S PR _ CT _ C _

Would you believe it?

A shopkeeper serves an older person when you have been waiting longer.

You will calm yourself by...

....

You think to yourself ....

....

You decide to ....

....

You spend a lot of time on your homework and the teacher forgets to collect it.

You will calm yourself by...

....

You think to yourself ....

....

You decide to ....

....

Think up an incident of your own and explain why you would be angry, how you would calm yourself and what you would do about it?

Session EIGHTEEN

KEEPING COOL

Purpose

To encourage students to keep events in perspective

To encourage students to seek solutions to life events.

Preparation

1.   Photocopy 'Keeping Cool' game, 'Keeping Cool' worksheet, and 'Calamitous Catastrophe' habit builder for each student.

2.   Provide enough dice for each student to have a turn at rolling.

Core Activity

1.   Distribute a 'Keeping Cool' game hand out to each student.

      Roll the dice twice; once to choose an event. Instruct students to write down how they would feel about this event.

2.   Roll the dice a second time to choose an emotional response. If 3 & 6 are rolled, the scenario will be: the television blows up and the response is one of excitement.

3.   Students then:

      ➢   Explain whether the response from rolling the dice was the same or different to their own response.

      ➢   Give a dolphin or shark thought that might cause the feeling they threw with their dice?

      ➢   Rate the event on the 'Feelings Barometer'?

      ➢   Say if they think it is a healthy or unhealthy response?

      ➢   If it is an unhealthy response, what might they do to protect against having this response?

4.   Distribute worksheet, 'Keeping Cool' and ask students to answer the questions about their incident.

5.   Ask students to write a story as described on hand out, 'Calamitous Catastrophe'.

————————<◆>————————

Discussion questions

Do you ever over react to something?

Why do you sometimes over react?

How might over reacting cause problems?

What can you do to stop yourself from over reacting?

In what ways is over reacting like being spun around in a chair?

(Add to the 'Perspective' list from session eleven.)

Keeping Cool Game

Response / Situation	Angry 1.	Happy 2.	Worried 3.	Scared 4.	Sad 5.	Excited 6.
1. A friend doesn't invite you to a party						
2. Your family take you on a long drive						
3. The television blows up						
4. Your family tell you that you are all moving to a different country						
5. A teacher tells you that you need to hand in some work by tomorrow						
6. Your family bring home a new pet for you and guess what, it's a pig.						

Keeping Cool

Event ....

Response...

Reason for Response

....

....

....

Would a different response have been better?

....

....

What might you think to have a different response?

....

....

**To discover the thought from Bunji unjumble the sentence
Kindly yourself always to speak.**

Calamitous Catastrophe

Write a story about an event and how it turned into
a huge catastrophe.

Courage

Purpose

To explore the notion of courage and how risk taking relates to it.

> Courage is a habit you learn through practice, just like other habits. To develop courage you need to care about things as well as believe in things. In other words, courageous people need a reason for being courageous.

Preparation

1. Make a 'Very Stupid' sign and a 'Very Courageous' sign.

2. Make up 'COURAGE CARDS" (see page 120).

3. Photocopy 'Courageous People' worksheet.

COURAGE cont....

Core Activity

1. Place a 'Very Stupid' sign at one end of the room and a 'Very Courageous' sign at the other end of the room.

2. Ask students to stand in a circle.

3. Distribute a 'courage card' to each student.

4. Ask students to read their card and to rate it from stupid to courageous. If it is a bit stupid and a bit courageous, it should go in the middle of the line. If it is mainly courageous, it should go closer to the 'Very Courageous' sign than the 'Very Stupid' sign.

5. Students should take turns in placing their cards along the continuum. When they place their cards they should give a reason for their placement.

6. Other students can say whether they agree or disagree.

7. When it is a student's turn, they can move other cards as long as they give a reason. You might help students to decide by advising them that:

   Courage is measured by:

   ➢ Level of risk

   ➢ Quality of purpose

If something has a high level of risk, but is for a bad purpose, it may be more stupid than courageous. If something has low risk, but an important purpose, it might be neither stupid or courageous, so it would rate in the middle. If something is high risk and for an important purpose, it might rate as very courageous.

8. Be aware to integrate the 'discussion questions' into the 'Courage rating continuum'.

9. Read the stories about 2 courageous women on the worksheet.

10. As a class, brainstorm a list of courageous people.

11. Discuss why these people are courageous?

    In pairs, ask students to tell each other of times when they have been courageous and explain why they had the strength to be courageous.

    Share the stories with the class.

Discussion questions

What is courage?

When do people display courage?

Are people born courageous, or do they learn to be courageous?

Why do people become courageous?

COURAGE CARDS

BRINGING YOUR TEDDY TO SCHOOL	GETTING A DIFFERENT HAIRCUT
PLAYING FOOTBALL	PLAYING NETBALL
SPEAKING UP FOR YOURSELF	SPEAKING UP FOR SOMEONE ELSE
WRITING LOVE POETRY	ASKING SOMEONE TO GO OUT WITH YOU
DOING YOUR HOMEWORK	NOT DOING YOUR HOMEWORK
ADMITTING YOU CAN'T DO SOMETHING	PUNCHING SOMEONE WHO IS ANNOYING YOU
DIVING OFF A HIGH TOWER	BUNJI JUMPING
RIDING A BIKE WITHOUT A HELMET	PERFORMING IN FRONT OF A LARGE AUDIENCE
STEALING FROM A SHOP	SMOKING A CIGARETTE
STANDING UP FOR SOMEONE WHO IS BEING BULLIED	SEEKING HELP FOR A PROBLEM

Courageous People

Read the short biographies of two great Australian women and decide whether they were/are courageous people. Consider their purpose and the risks they were taking.

Caroline Chisholm (1808 - 1877).

Born in England, she came to Australia in 1838 when living conditions were very squalid, and many people lived in poverty. Women were often badly treated and had few rights. Caroline Chisholm, with the support and admiration of her husband, committed herself to a life serving other women.

Some of her better known achievements included setting up a home for poor women, the arranging of free trips for the families of convicts to join them in Australia and tireless efforts to improve the conditions on the ships that brought people to Australia.

By the end of her life, Caroline Chisholm had helped many thousands of Australians, especially women. She died with very little money or assets. She had served others without thought of her own well-being, and at a time when support from others was hard to find.

Shirley Smith (1921 - 1998).

Suffering from epilepsy, Shirley was educated at home by her grandfather. She could speak many aboriginal languages but never learned to read or write in English.

In spite of her lack of English language skills, she was a great friend to aboriginal people who were in trouble with the law. She would accompany them to court and visit them in prison. She played an important role in the creation of the Aboriginal Medical Service and the Aboriginal Legal Service. She became affectionately known as 'Mama Shirl' because of her dedication to aboriginal people who were in trouble.

Think of someone you think is courageous.

Explain why you think they are courageous.

Give an example of something they have done that is courageous.

To discover the thought from Bunji fill in the words

D_ TH _ NGS TH _ T M _ TT _ R

THE FUTURE GAZERS

GREETINGS FROM MANNS BEACH

Purpose

This session helps students to set educational goals and to make plans for the future.

Preparation

Precautions: During all guided imagery/relaxation/visualisation activities there is a risk that particular people may experience some discomfort due to lowered blood pressure. A lowering of blood pressure may cause sensations of dizziness, light-headedness or nausea. People who are hypoglycaemic or who have not eaten for some hours may be especially vulnerable.

If this occurs it is advisable to ask the person to lie down in a comfortable place and to place a cushion or pillow under their feet (to raise their feet above the level of their torso). Providing a sweet biscuit can also assist in raising blood sugar levels.

If symptoms persist for longer than 20 minutes seek medical or nursing advice.

For 'The Mountain of Dreams':

1. Collect chips for each player to use as a marker.

2. Photocopy for each group, a 'Mountain of Dreams' sheet (join two pages together), a set of 'Choice cards' and an 'Umpire Directions sheet'.

3. Cut the cards into squares.

4. Photocopy 'Postcards from your Future' worksheet and 'My Fabulous Future' habit builder.

Core Activity

1. Ask students to find a comfortable position and read from the 'visualisation activity' on the following page, softly and slowly.

2. Discuss questions.

3. Divide students into groups of 3 – 6.

4. Hand out 'The Mountain of Dreams' game and distribute a dice to each group.

5. Ask for a volunteer from each group to be the 'umpire'.

6. Rules of the game.

   a) Students take turns to throw the dice.

   b) For each throw, they progress along the track by the number on the dice.

   c) If they land on a black square, they select a choice card from the top of the pile. On the choice card will be a description of an event or a feeling. The player must choose one of the responses a, b or c. They should choose the response which is most likely to help them reach the summit. When the player has made a choice, the 'umpire' looks up their answer on the 'Umpire Directions sheet'. The player then moves as directed.

   d) The winner is the first player to reach the summit.

7. Have a class collection of postcards and pin them around the class. Ask students to choose one that they would like to receive from themselves in the future. Ask students to complete the 'Postcards from Your Future' worksheet.

8. Encourage students to set themselves three goals on their 'My Fabulous Future' habit builder sheet.

9. Make a time to meet with students (and their parents if possible) to discuss their progress toward their goals.

Discussion questions

For Visualisation Activity:

What was the special gift?

Why was this a special gift?

Will this gift make your life easier or harder?

How did you feel when you had your eyes closed?

For 'The Mountain of Dreams':

Brainstorm the qualities people need to reach their goals?

How important is perseverance?

Is it courageous to dare to 'Hope'?

Visualisation Activity

" Now I want everyone to take some time off from what they are doing and to find a comfortable position to sit in. You may like to put your head on the desk (or table) in front of you and close your eyes. If you want to move to make yourself even more comfortable or open your eyes at any time you may. As you close your eyes and begin to take some time away from the rush and bustle of the school day, I wonder if you can go on an imaginary trip into outer space. ...

With your eyes closed, I wonder if you can imagine that you can fly safely for a time... and that as you breathe easily and deeply, you can begin to imagine that you start to float up away from the school into the fresh sweet air outside and even though it may feel strange at first... you can look down as you move away from school. As you look down you can see the tops of houses and trees and by moving a shoulder you can begin to move in that direction.

As you float up into the atmosphere you begin to gain speed and start to move through the clouds. Almost before you know it, you are above the clouds and in the beautiful sunshine and heading into space. At all times you can feel comfortable and breathe calmly and easily.

As you gain even more speed, you find that you can move easily by moving one shoulder to go in one direction and the other shoulder to go in the other. Even as you fly into space you find that you can turn around and see the beauty of the earth... the clouds drifting over oceans and forests... areas of red desert and mountain ranges and areas of lush green... going further into space you begin to see asteroids and planets and as you fly at incredible speeds you flick past planets and moons and comets. In the distance you begin to see a planet that takes your interest. This planet is even more interesting than it seems at first and you slow down to land on it.

As you enter its atmosphere you notice that it is similar to earth but not exactly the same. There are some surprising differences and I don't know whether it will be the colours or the land shapes or the quality of the light that you will begin to notice first. The air on this planet is also very special and as you breathe deeply and calmly you can notice a feeling of relaxation and well-being.

One of the interesting aspects of this planet is that it has time zones. So if you move one way, you will find that you are a year younger. Notice what it feels like to be younger. You may be able to feel differently than you do usually. As you begin to move in the other direction you suddenly notice that you become precisely one year older. Notice how you feel. What changes can you see? As you do, so a wise person comes up to you. This person is safe and helpful and hands you a package and tells you that in the package is a gift from the future- a talent or skill that you will need and enjoy- and to look in the package and to look closely. Take some time now to think about the package and the wise figure's words and then prepare to return to earth. Start to float up into the atmosphere and into space. You begin to gain speed and as you do so you pass planets and comets and as earth comes back in sight you speed around in a large arc, in celebration of your new skills and then re-enter the earth's atmosphere. Seeing Australia below you, red and green you return slowly to your starting point and in you own time as you begin to feel ready start to open your eyes .5...4...3...2..1. open your eyes and come back into the room now."

THE MOUNTAIN OF DREAMS

DIRECTIONS

1. You need one dice and a marker for each player, and you need to appoint an umpire.

2. The object of the game is to successfully climb the mountain by reaching the finish.

3. If you land on a BLACK square, you need to pick up a 'CHOICE CARD'. Read it and, using the 'UMPIRE DIRECTIONS SHEET', choose what you would do.

4. Tell the umpire your choice and he/she will instruct you to move forward, backward or to stay where you are, depending on your choice.

5. The winner is the first person to reach the finish.

HINT: Be positive in your response

FINISH

78
77
75
74
72
71
65
67
68
69
64
62
61
50
52
54
59
49
48
46
55
58
45
57
38
39
40
43
42
28
27
25
24
18
20
21
22

CHOICE CARDS

Choose the answer that is most likely to help you reach the summit.

1. A storm is coming

A) You prepare for the worst but hope for the best

B) You keep going and hope for the best

C) You panic and flee for the base camp

2. You get angry and tell another climber to "Get Lost"

A) You forget about it and move on

B) You apologise and explain why you were angry

C) You know you had every right to be angry.

3. You climb the most difficult cliff face. You tell Yourself

A) You were lucky

B) If you can do that the rest will be easy.

C) You must keep doing your best till the end.

4. One of the climbers quits

A) You make new plans

B) You give up

C) You make jokes about how the "scaredy cat" quit

5. You get frustrated with the slow progress

A) You yell at everybody and tell them to hurry up

B) You keep your feelings to yourself

C) You discuss your feelings with the other climbers

6. You lose some equipment

A) You improvise to replace it

B) You sit down and cry

C) You do without

7. The other climbers give plenty of compliments

A) You lap it up

B) You know they don't mean it

C) You give compliments to them

8. You feel tired

A) You have a sleep in

B) You take a pill

C) You eat high energy food

CHOICE CARDS

Choose the answer that is most likely to help you reach the summit.

9. You push yourself beyond what you thought was possible
A) You brag about how good you are
B) You expect a pat on the back
C) You feel incredibly positive

10. You are injured
A) You consider how uncomfortable it is
B) You think about what could have happened
C) You tell everybody it didn't hurt because you are tough

11. Nobody notices how important you are
A) You start calling everybody names
B) You tell them
C) You reassure yourself by writing it in your diary

12. You lose contact with base camp
A) You worry about ever seeing it again
B) You discuss how it affects safety
C) You set off flares to let them know you are alive

13. The view is spectacular
A) You are too busy too look at it
B) You feel great
C) You are pleased to be a climber

14. You begin to have second thoughts
A) You begin to dwell on your fears
B) You think of the summit
C) You force yourself to think about what to do next

15. You become frightened when you stare at the summit
A) You stop staring at it
B) You begin to think you won't make it
C) You go to the toilet

16. You are scared of the highest and hardest stage that lies ahead
A) You stop thinking about it
B) You eat lollies to cheer you up
C) You talk to someone who has climbed it before

THE FUTURE GAZERS cont....

CHOICE CARDS

Choose the answer that is most likely to help you reach the summit.

17. Your fitness is getting better A) You take the day off B) You practise harder C) You eat ice cream and lollies	**18. You have all the right gear** A) You practise using it B) You brag about it to the other climbers C) You know you will be alright
19. You have a fight with another team member A) You decide you hate them B) You ignore them C) You discuss ways of avoiding more arguments	**20. You have a fear of heights** A) You practise until you overcome it B) You give up C) You don't look down

❮◆❯

UMPIRE DIRECTIONS SHEET

Go forward, back or stay where you are depending on the direction
you are given for your answer

1. **A storm is coming.**
   A) go forward 2   B) go back 1   C) go back to base camp

2. **You get angry and tell another climber to "Get Lost"**
   A) stay where you are   B) stay where you are   C) go back 1

3. **You climb the most difficult cliff face. You tell yourself:**
   A) stay where you are   B) go back one   C) go forward 2

4. **One of the climbers quits**
   A) stay where you are   B) go back to the start   C) go back 1

5. **You get frustrated with the slow progress**
   A) go back 1   B) stay where you are   C) go forward 1

6. **You lose some equipment**
   A) go forward 1   B) go back 1   C) stay where you are

7. **The other climbers give plenty of compliments**
   A) stay where you are   B) go back 1   C) go forward 1

8. **You feel tired**
   A) stay where you are   B) go back 1   C) go forward 1

9. **You push yourself beyond what you thought was possible**
   A) stay where you are   B) go back 1   C) go forward 3

10. **You are injured**
    A) stay where you are   B) go back 1   C) go back 1

UMPIRE DIRECTIONS SHEET

Go forward, back or stay where you are depending on the direction you are given for your answer

11. Nobody notices how important you are
A) go back 3   B) stay where you are   C) go forward 1

12. You lose contact with base camp
A) go back 1   B) stay where you are   C) stay where you are

13. The view is spectacular.
A) stay where you are   B) go forward 1   C) go forward 1

14. You have second thoughts
A) go back 2   B) go forward   C) go forward 1

15. You become frightened when you stare at the summit
A) stay where you are   B) go back 2   C) stay where you are

16. You are scared by the highest and hardest stage that lies ahead
A) stay where you are   B) stay where you are   C) go forward 2

17. Your fitness is improving
A) go back 1   B) go forward 2   C) stay where you are

18. You have all the right equipment
A) go forward 1   B) go back 1   C) stay where you are

19. You have a fight with another team member
A) go back 1   B) go back 1   C) stay where you are

20. You have a fear of heights
A) advance 2   B) go back to base camp   C) stay where you are

Postcards from your future

Where would you like it to be from?

What would you like it to say?

What would you need to take with you?

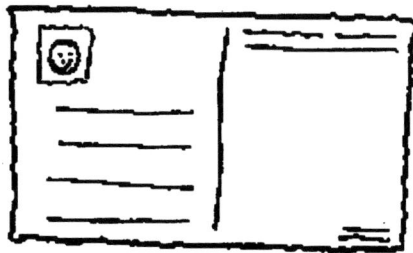

To discover the final thought from Bunji, unjumble the final word.
YOU ARE ATERG!

My Fabulous Future

Three goals I would like to achieve this term are:

1..
....
....
....

2..
....
....
....

3..
....
....
....

These goals should be agreed with your parents and teacher. At regular intervals, you should meet with your teacher and parents to discuss your progress toward your goals.
They may be able to help you.

Once you have achieved your goals, you can set some new ones.

Evaluation Tools

EVALUATION TOOLS

Assessment Of Emotional Intelligence and Resilience- Extensive

Behaviours	Rating		
	Beginning	Consolidating	Established
1. Demonstrates empathy to others			
2. Can identify supportive people they know			
3. Can connect with peers			
4. Can join in with others			
5. Can read non-verbal cues in others			
6. Can interpret tones of voice			
7. Can read emotional intent in visual materials such as paintings, faces			
8. Can read emotional intent in auditory materials such as music			
9. Can describe their own feelings			
10. Can express a variety of feelings			
11. Can identify personal strengths			
12. Can identify activities that make them feel good			
13. Can identify activities that make them feel unhappy			
14. Can consider the qualities of friendship			
15. Can give compliments to others			
16. Can identify positive thoughts			
17. Can identify negative thoughts			
18. Can identify the triggers for anger			
19. Can calm themselves down			
20. Can take different perspectives of the same event			
21. Aware of bullying and its negative consequences			
22. Can develop personal goals			
23. Can identify a positive future			
24. Can develop an action plan for achieving goals			
25. Can have fun			

EVALUATION TOOLS

Assessment Of Emotional Intelligence

Core Skills and Habits	Rating		
	Beginning	Consolidating	Established
Demonstrates an ability to read the emotional cues in others: read non-verbal cues, interpret tones of voice, read emotional intent in visual materials such as paintings faces and auditory materials such as music.			
Demonstrates an ability to label and express own emotions appropriately: can describe their own feelings, able to express a variety of feelings, identify personal strengths and activities that make them feel good. Able to develop personal goals and identify a positive future, able to develop an action plan for achieving goals and to have fun.			
Demonstrates an ability to calm or regulate emotions: able to identify positive thoughts, able to identify negative thoughts, able to identify the triggers for anger, able to calm themselves down, able to take different perspectives of the same event.			
Demonstrates an ability to connect well with others: joins in with others, connects with peers, demonstrates empathy to others, can identify supportive people they know, able to consider the qualities of friendship, able to give compliments to others, awareness of bullying and its negative consequences.			

Please note: the ability of each person to show the behaviours described in both of the assessment charts varies greatly with development and environment.

Awards
Ideas &
Puzzles

RESILIENT PERSON AWARD

This is to Certify That

....

Has Completed
The HEART MASTERS Program

Signed ....

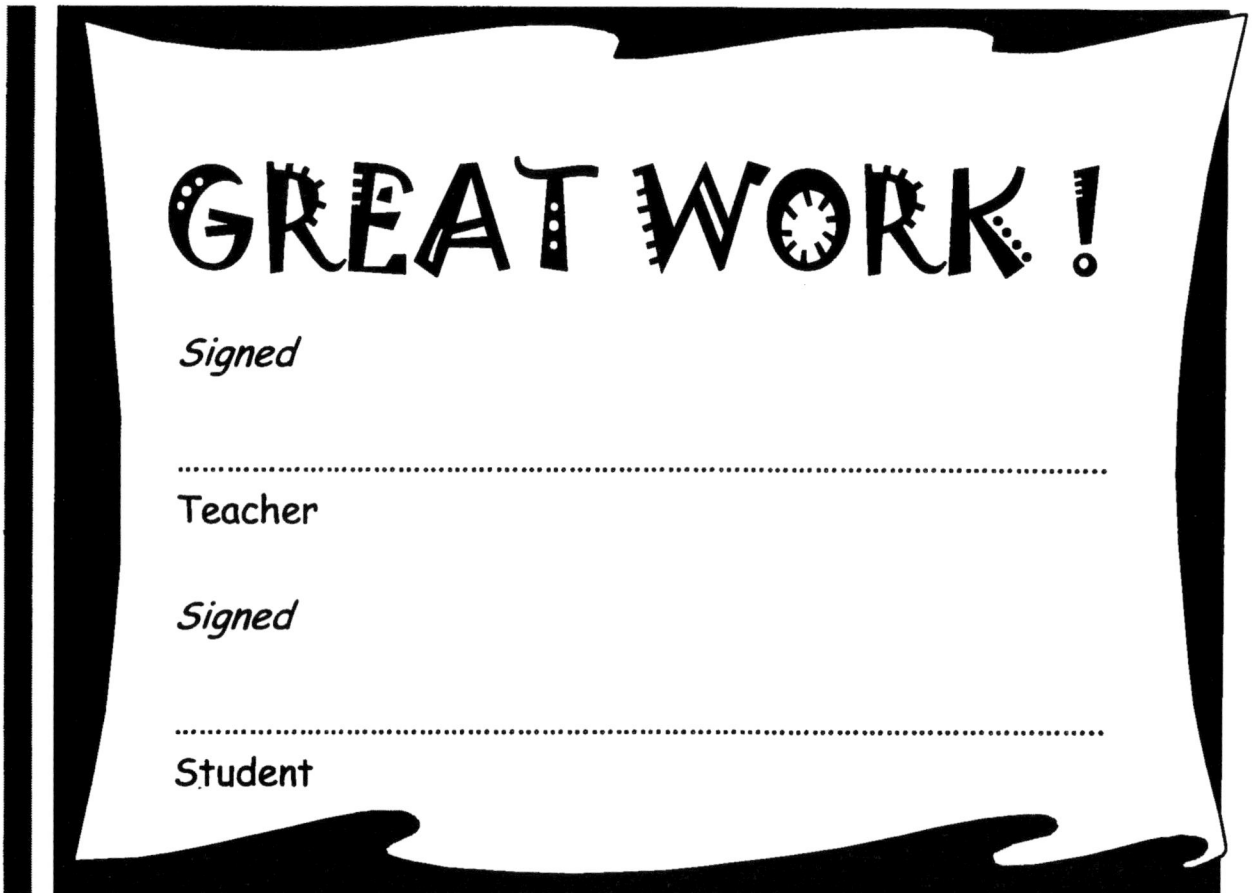

GREAT WORK !

Signed

....

Teacher

Signed

....

Student

WORD SEARCH
FIND THE FEELING

D	L	I	V	E	L	V	Q	E	I	U	X	M	S
P	E	S	G	S	B	T	U	K	I	N	D	U	T
O	X	L	A	U	G	H	I	N	G	B	O	O	H
L	C	E	I	O	U	I	E	Q	T	I	R	E	D
I	I	E	H	G	R	R	T	Q	R	N	K	X	E
T	T	D	M	D	H	S	F	U	P	T	J	C	U
E	E	Y	T	E	Y	T	C	G	A	E	L	I	O
P	O	F	U	N	N	Y	E	A	I	S	N	T	N
Z	O	D	M	B	O	R	E	D	R	T	M	E	N
X	B	L	N	R	E	L	I	E	V	E	D	D	H
C	K	D	E	T	H	G	I	L	E	D	D	H	A
I	R	R	I	T	A	T	E	D	Y	P	P	A	H
K	M	T	S	B	E	A	M	U	S	E	D	S	G
F	E	A	R	F	U	L	D	E	I	R	R	O	U

Find these 'feeling' words:

HAPPY	EXCITED	ANNOYED	DELIGHTED	WORRIED
POLITE	IRRITATED	FRIENDLY	FUNNY	FEARFUL
AMUSED	KIND	INTERESTED	BORED	TIRED
LIVELY	RELIEVED	THIRSTY	HUNGRY	SLEEPY
QUIET	LAUGHING	SCARED	CURIOUS	

MATCH THE FEELING TO THE FACE

TIRED

CURIOUS

SCARED

WORRIED

DELIGHTED

THIRSTY

UNJUMBLE THESE WORDS

Dbreo	
Yilvel	
Nikd	
Euqti	
Ppahy	
Yhunrg	
Lyiefrdn	
Diewrro	
Nfyun	
Suouirc	

HOW MANY WORDS CAN YOU MAKE OUT OF ...

Heart Master?	Peace Maker?	Future Gazer?	Bouncing Bunji?

Personal Best

Personal Best

A Programme for the development of personal mastery and self-esteem

Purpose

The Personal Best is a programme that allows each student to take on a project of their choosing and to develop it with supervision and consultation from their teacher. The project will run over one term and time will be set aside for each student to individually meet with a staff member.

Personal Best is based on research indicating that experiences of personal mastery and competence bolster self-esteem.

The programme requires staff to take on the role of coaches who meet individually with each student to set goals, to review progress and to expand the project. Parents can be invited to take on a role as a Personal Best Facilitation Staff member who will meet with small groups of students undertaking projects.

Aim of Personal Best

The aim of Personal Best is for each student to have an experience taking on a project of interest and to then set goals regarding that project, implement the project, have it reviewed with constructive feedback and to then incorporate that feedback and to expand the project.

Aims

➢ For each student to have an experience of taking on a project of interest

➢ Students learn to set goals

➢ Students learn to set implementation plans and carry them out

➢ Learn to review / evaluate

➢ Experience personal success

➢ Experience positive learning outcomes

➢ Transpose learning for the project to other learning experiences

Presentation and Celebration

➢ Exhibition and celebration of project and achievements / experiences

➢ Parents / friends / coaches are invited to attend an assembly at the commencement of the programme and a celebratory evening / afternoon where all work is displayed and certificates presented to students. They can also be invited to facilitate a group of students undertaking an activity.

Implementation

➢ Staff and other significant mentors take on the role of PB coaches.

➢ Staff meet students individually to set goals, review progress, further develop plans.

➢ Curriculum facilitation- allow for time to be used during classes

➢ Curriculum links made - benefits from the programme and students learning experiences are transferred into their academic learning in the school environment.

Timeline

Week 1

➢ Guidelines established

➢ Documentation prepared

Week 2

➢ Staff meets - initial planning - establish facilitation teachers

➢ Letters home re project / time out of class / assembly (invite parents)

Week 3

➢ Personal Best Launch Day held commencing with assembly

➢ Planning meetings conducted in home groups with facilitation teacher

➢ Implementation time allowed

Week 4

➢ Meetings between students and coaches occur and follow up meeting times are set

Week 5 & 6

➢ Implementation time

Week 7

➢ Preparation for presentation with facilitation teacher

➢ Implementation time

➢ Invitations to celebrations sent home

Week 8

➢ Final interviews, details for exhibition finalised and advertised

➢ Implementation time

Week 9

➢ Exhibition / celebration of work

➢ Commences with assembly then presentations occur in groups

Initial Communication with Students

> ➤ Distribute letters regarding PB programme launch via facilitation teacher
>
> ➤ Parents invited to attend assembly and morning tea on day of launch

Personal Best Facilitation Staff

Purpose

Personal Best Facilitation staff act as a primary staff member to co-ordinate a group of students. The programme aims to help students reach their personal best in the pursuit of goals they have set for themselves. Personal Best Facilitation staff may or may not be the personal best coach for all students in a group. It would be preferable for a facilitator to coach no more than approximately 6-8 students since meetings with students need to be fairly regular. Motivation, guidance, encouragement and a genuine interest are required.

Guidelines

➤ facilitate information about the programme to students and other staff

➤ liaise with students to establish selection of project, setting of goals, implementation plans

➤ encourage students throughout the project

➤ act as a guide for effective review of progress / achievements

➤ meet regularly with students as defined in the timeline and arrange additional meetings as required by individual students

➤ facilitate the presentation to staff, students and parents

➤ facilitate the exhibition / celebration of achievements

➤ have at least one conversation with each about their project that they are not expecting

Personal Best Coaches

Purpose

The programme aims to enable students to reach their personal best in the pursuit of goals they set for themselves. In accepting the role of a Personal Best Coach for a student (s) you become their primary support person throughout their endeavour. It would be preferable for you to coach no more than 6-8 students as you need to meet with them fairly regularly to facilitate the level of encouragement and mentoring involved.

Guidelines

➢ liaise with students to establish selection of project, setting of goals, implementation plans.

➢ encourage students throughout the project

➢ act as a guide for effective review of progress / achievements

➢ meet regularly with students as often as they require, a minimum number of meetings should be scheduled at the outset

➢ provide support throughout the project - various forms of this will develop according to the needs of your students

➢ provide support for the exhibition / celebration of achievement

➢ have at least one conversation with each student in your group that they are not expecting about their project

➢ lead by example - share your own personal best programme with students

Goal Setting Form

Name:

Personal Best Co-ordinating Teacher:

Personal Best Coach:

AIMS OF THE PROJECT

* To learn about yourself

* To learn how to set and achieve goals

* To experience decision making

* To solve problems

* To respond to challenges

* To review effectiveness

* To acknowledge achievement

Task

You are to choose a project that interests you where you can work to achieve your personal best (consider your interests / strengths / weaknesses).

The opportunities are endless.

This is your individual project. Good Luck!

Brief Description of Project

Goals

1.

2.

3.

Main Anticipated Outcome:

Review Date: Week 5

Signed ....

Personal Best

About Me

MY INTERESTS	MY STRENGTHS	THINGS I CAN IMPROVE ON

Project Ideas

Personal Best Project Menu

Suggestions

1. Create a magazine on your favourite sport

2. Write a play / television show / story on a topic of your choosing

3. Develop a series of school policies and interview a series of staff and students about the rules you would have in an " ideal" school

4. Develop a good food guide for kids (survey students about food choices and develop suggested menus)

5. Survey a class group about different musical tastes and write a report on this.

6. Create an artistic representation of the school as a series of pictures or sculptures

7. Set a goal to achieve a certain level of skill or competency at a task (sport, artistic talent)

8. Develop a survey for local council

9. Develop a business idea

10. Establish business links with Rotary and Lions Clubs

11. Develop a community portrait (photo montage)

12. Survey parents of the school about expectations, how they are going to celebrate the end of the year

13. Develop a "what you really need to know" guide for new students

14. Write and perform a piece of music

15. Develop a presentation around a type of music eg. movement / dance piece

16. Create community awareness of an issue that is important to you

17. Prepare a presentation about the world in the year 2010

Personal Best - Implementation Form

Name:

Personal Best Co-ordinating Teacher:

Personal Best Coach:

Project Title:

Goals	Strategies to Achieve Goal	Expected Outcome	Date

Exhibition / Presentation of Work

Outline how you will present your work in the final week of term.